D0407988

HOW TO SAY NO TO A RAPIST AND SURVIVE

Frederic Storaska

HOW TO SAY NO TO A RAPIST AND SURVIVE

Random House
New York

Library of Congress Cataloging in Publication Data

Storaska, Frederic, 1942–
How to say no to a rapist and survive.

Bibliography: p. 233
1. Rape—United States—Prevention.
I. Title.
HV6561.S85   364.4   74-22123
ISBN 0-394-49579-9

Manufactured in the United States of America

23456789

FIRST EDITION

*To all the eleven-year-old girls
who have had to endure the hell
that a negligent society allows*

Acknowledgments

The support of the following people and groups was basic to my rape prevention program, and thus this book: the dozens of police officers throughout North Carolina who helped me with my initial research; Shannon Phillips, Ralph J. Andrews, and Dr. William Friday, who believed and encouraged a twenty-two-year-old with ideas only and no proof; Dr. Harold Miller and Dr. James Cole, who gave me the primary tool to combat rape—understanding people; Hayward Starling, who first showed me the proof of my program and encouraged me to make sure as many women as possible heard it; the hundreds of deans of women and Associated Women Students' officers who were interested in preventing rape before such concern became fashionable; the thousands of women who had enough confidence and trust in me to relate their personal experiences; Carlton Sedgeley, who provided guidance; Wilbur Rykert, Doyle Shackelford, Lt. Mary Keefe, Sgt. Harry O'Reilly, and Ralph F. Garofalo who shared their expertise with me in editing this book; the many friends and associates who so willingly offered their advice, suggestions, and services; my mother and father, who helped by just being themselves; my two sons, Bret and Todd, who donated their time with me; but most of all to Betty Lou, my partner in life, without whose boundless patience, understanding, and support this book and my rape prevention program would not be a reality.

A special note: I want to thank writer Harvey A. Ardman for his help in the organizing and writing of this book.

Contents

In the Beginning:
An Introduction

Early one evening in the summer of 1964, after completing some casework on juvenile delinquency in a Southern city and returning to my car, I glanced into an alley, and to my horror, found a gang of young teenagers raping and beating an eleven-year-old girl.

I saw red. Being young and not too cautious (I was a college junior at the time) and knowing karate, I stormed into the gang, kicking and flailing away at the girl's attackers.

Fortunately, most of them—there were about ten or eleven, I guess—were on the scrawny side, but then in my mood anybody would have looked scrawny. And they weren't interested in doing battle with an enraged karate-ist, a lineman on his college football team who was four inches taller and fifty pounds heavier than most of them. They ran, those who could. The rest, strewn about, didn't move.

I didn't try to follow. The girl was my main concern. I lifted her up and carried her back to her parents' house.

She was battered, bruised and, thank God, dazed. After a while, she recovered from her injuries—though she carries the scars to this day. So do I. That sickening incident was one of the most profound experiences of my life. It affects me even now. No child, no woman, no human being should ever have to undergo what happened to that young girl.

Despite my knowledge of karate, despite my size and strength, I'd been powerless to prevent the attack on that eleven-year-old girl. Oh, I suppose if I'd been walking beside her from the beginning, that gang might have let her alone. But there's no way to provide every woman walking alone (or driving a car, or sitting in her house or apartment) with a constant companion, a protector ready—and able—to defend her against an assaulter or group of assaulters.

The more I thought about it, the more I realized that as long as society is the way it is, the only person who could prevent rape was the woman herself. Alone. Somehow, there had to be a way that *all* women—young or old, weak or strong, timid or bold—could either sidestep an attack or successfully deal with their assaulters. And it had to be a technique that didn't primarily depend upon physical self-defense, such as karate, judo or jujitsu, or on weapons, since turning every woman in the United States into a black belt or a soldier just wasn't realistic.

I spent my last years of college looking for this technique and I've never had a more frustrating time. My search of the literature on assault revealed that no one had developed a method by which the average woman could defend herself against rape. Actually, it didn't even seem as if anyone was trying to develop a method. In fact, very few people had written about the subject at all. Books on rape or the victims of rape or the rapist were scarce. Most available information was limited to a few dozen scholarly monographs in psychiatric, psychological or sociological journals, plus a small number of foreign works. Almost without exception, the published material on rape dwelt not on rape prevention but on the make-up of the rapist. Each monograph examined one tiny slice of the rapist's life—his childhood, his upbringing, his early sexual experiences, his marital woes, his mental stability. Not one offered any help to the potential victim. Even in recent years, when a great deal more has been written on the subject, interest has tended to focus on what to do after you're raped, rather than on how to prevent rape.

It gradually occurred to me that if there were ever going to be a program women could use to protect themselves against assault, it would have to be developed from scratch. I set out to meet this need. Fortunately, I was in an unusually good position to get more information. As one of the few holders of a black belt in karate in the Southeast at the time, I had been helping to pay my college expenses by teaching self-defense karate to members of the U.S. Treasury Department, the North Carolina Highway Patrol, and the police and sheriff's departments of Raleigh, Durham, Greensboro, Winston-Salem and several other cities. Now I went to some of my police contacts to learn all they could tell me.

Soon another source of information opened up for me. I'd been lecturing on self-defense at local recreation departments, Y's, high schools and a few universities, incorporating into my talks my fledgling ideas and theories on rape prevention. To my surprise, women began to come up to me after my lectures—women who had been assaulted both recently and many years before—to tell me how they'd tried to handle the attack and whether their tactics had succeeded or failed. These women came to me desperately needing to talk to someone who would be empathetic, and also hoping to ease some of the guilt they felt about not reporting the assault. I would fit this new information into what I already knew about rape prevention and use it in succeeding lectures.

Finally, a private women's college called me and invited me to lecture not on self-defense but solely on rape prevention. There had been several assaults in recent months in the area and they urgently wanted to give their students some way to protect themselves before something happened on *their* campus. I put my knowledge and my theories together and told those young women everything I knew about preventing assaults or surviving them with the least possible injury. But I knew my theories were just that: educated guesses on how to ward off the assaulter or minimize the danger of bodily harm. The only thing I was really sure about at that time was that what I advocated—even if it didn't help them—wouldn't hurt them.

It's not often that a man has his theories so quickly and positively confirmed as I did after I gave that first lecture on rape prevention ten years ago. Twelve weeks later, in a court trial for rape a young woman testified for the prosecution that the advice I gave in my lecture had saved her life. Her statement was verified by the chief investigating agent of the state bureau of investigation. And six months later, when another young woman was murdered during an assault on a nearby campus, the same chief investigating agent told me that if the young woman had heard my lecture she, too, would probably have survived the assault.

Since then, I have lectured on rape prevention in every state in the continental United States. Many colleges at which I speak schedule the program on a regular basis. Over the past ten years, I have received documented evidence that my lectures have either prevented serious assaults or saved lives in two hundred and seventy-three cases, and it is very probable that there are hundreds of other cases in which the assault was avoided before it became serious enough to report, or where the information simply never filtered back to me.

Thousands of women and even men, over 4000, have spent long hours telling me of the assaults they've experienced and how they've dealt with them. I want to thank those victims of assaults who have so generously shared their experiences with me and have allowed me to use both their successes and failures to help complete my system. I have used these case histories in this book—with names deleted and circumstances disguised, for the sake of privacy—so that others can benefit.

I believe that every woman has the absolute right not to be raped. I wrote this book to explain what rape is, what happens during the assault, what the rapist wants and needs, and how to deal with the assault situation. I wrote it because I was sick of seeing and hearing about women being raped, attacked, killed and mutilated. I wrote it because I was disgusted that nobody was doing anything about the problem, and because in most places in America, rape was a taboo subject and what passed for rape education was nothing more than ostrich-imitation or scare tactics. And I also wrote it in the hope of encouraging others to come forward to help us understand and prevent rape and assault.

HOW TO SAY NO TO A RAPIST AND SURVIVE

What Do You Mean—"Rape"?

Over the years, I've learned that everyone has his own definition of rape. Your Aunt Minnie may quite sincerely believe she's being raped when a vagrant accosts her on the street and demands a dime, or whatever the going rate is these days, for a cup of coffee. Your Uncle Archie might be convinced it's rape when he finds out that his sixteen-year-old daughter Sally has been making like a bunny with her eighteen-year-old boyfriend Ralph.

Depending on which dictionary you read, rape may be anything from abduction to abusive treatment to the taking of *anything* by force. Even legal definitions of the act differ from state to state. Rape is usually defined in the statutes as "unlawful carnal knowledge of a woman by force and without her consent." By carnal knowledge, the statute writers mean sexual intercourse. And the sexual intercourse needn't be "complete." Even the slightest entry of the penis into the vagina qualifies. The man need not climax.

In some states, if the woman is unconscious, drugged or

dead drunk, if she is simply unable to either consent or protest, the man who has sexual intercourse with her is raping her. And in a few states, a man who commits sexual intercourse by means of deception is also considered a rapist. That might happen if, in the middle of the night, a stranger crawls into a woman's bed, and pretending to be her husband, has sex with her.

In some jurisdictions it's rape only if the assaulter uses actual force on his victim and if she resists him physically. And believe it or not, in several states it's rape only if the assaulter uses actual force on his victim, and she resists and fights with every available means *and* someone else, a third person, is present to corroborate all the above. In others, the threat of force is sufficient, when combined with the victim's unwillingness—whether or not she states it. And just about everywhere in the United States, it's rape when a man has intercourse with a girl under the age of sixteen, even if she's begged for sexual intercourse on bended knee.

In most places, there's just no way a man can rape his wife. Legally, anyhow, she must submit to him whenever he wants her to. (Of course, there's no law that says a woman has to stay married to a man who treats her as a convenience, not a person.)

To my way of thinking, the only practical definition of rape is "forcible sexual intercourse." If you're a woman, and you have sexual intercourse when you don't want to be having sexual intercourse, that's rape. (And only the woman can ascertain when this is happening.) That's what this book is intended to prevent, along with the injuries and indignities that accompany the act.

Sexual intercourse isn't necessarily the only thing that happens during rape. In fact, for many women, it may be the most bearable part of the experience. The rapist may also insist on various other sexual acts—fellatio, genital fondling, anal intercourse and anything else within the limits of his imagination. To this he sometimes may add a beating, maiming or murder.

But the main event in rape, physically, is sexual intercourse, which is something you may be delighted to have —under other circumstances. So what the rapist wants from you is not a terrible thing at all, in itself. Many people think it's one of life's great pleasures. What's bad about rape is that you're being *forced* into intimacy against your will.

The writer Sanche de Gramont said it well. He wrote, "The man who commits rape is stealing something from the woman, something that is only precious when it is freely given; so that in the very act of stealing it, he is depreciating it. Even if he does not harm her physically, he is debasing the central feminine function."

Because rape is so intertwined with femininity, some women think no men, no matter how empathetic they might be, can ever truly understand the shock and sense of violation a woman feels when she's raped. As long as we have two sexes, I'll admit that there can't be an exact parallel. But men are subject to an act that produces similar feelings of shock and violation in homosexual rape. (And I'm not passing judgment on homosexuals here, only on rapists, whatever their sexual preference.) Any man who thinks a woman should "relax and enjoy" being raped should be forced to watch the homosexual rape scene in the movie *Deliverance* three or four times. That should produce an abundance of empathy.

Rape is certainly one of the worst things that can happen to a woman, but I believe that it isn't *the* worst. To put rape in first place, you'd have to ignore death, mutilation, disease, loss of a loved one, amputation of a limb, going blind, deafness or being mute, mental illness, paralysis and perhaps a few other catastrophes. All of these, I think, are worse than rape, and almost every woman I've talked with agrees. Still, I'll never forget the mother who came up to me after one lecture and told me she'd rather have her daughter dead than raped. I'm afraid I wasn't very nice to her. I told her I was glad I wasn't her daughter—or son, for that matter.

Mind you, when I say that rape isn't the worst thing that can happen to you, I'm not trying to dismiss it. It is a terrible experience, one to be avoided if at all possible. I'm just trying to put it into perspective, to remove some of the unreasoning terror attached to the word. If I could get everyone to agree, I'd stop using the word "rape" altogether and substitute, say, "penetration," or any other word that doesn't carry with it that immediate note of terror.

The terror comes, I think, from the many garish news stories of women who have been raped and murdered. The word "rape" automatically calls to mind the Boston Strangler or the Chicago nurses' tragedy. Yet my studies show that 2,168 out of every 2,169 women who are raped *aren't* murdered, no matter what impression you've gotten from the newspapers. It's just that the women who are "merely" raped, or "only" raped and beaten, don't make good copy, in the same way that the car accident resulting in two dented fenders isn't likely to make the papers, while the head-on crash that kills six will be featured on page one.

Not only are most rape victims not murdered, the vast majority aren't injured beyond the sexual assault. According to *Crimes of Violence*, a staff report of the National Commission on the Causes and Prevention of Violence, 76 percent of the victims of reported rapes weren't hurt. Of the remainder, 17.7 percent were injured not by weapons but by fist blows or kicks, 1.4 percent were injured by guns, 0.7 percent by knives and 0.6 percent by blunt instruments. Many rapes are reported only because women must have their injuries treated. The Commission has no figures on unreported rapes, of course, but my files show that injuries in these cases are very rare. And it is estimated that unreported rapes outnumber those reported to the authorities by anywhere from four to one to fifty to one. Actually, I think the ratio may be even higher than a hundred to one.

The sociologist Menachem Amir, who intensively studied all the reported rapes in Philadelphia during a single year, confirms the National Commission figures in his book *Patterns of Forcible Rape* (University of Chicago Press, 1971). He says that 87 percent of the time the rapist used only verbal coercion to subdue his victim. And when force was used, half the time it involved nothing more (?) than manhandling or beating. Now, that's not nice, but it isn't the same as being shot or stabbed.

Another reason for the fear connected with the word "rape" is the widespread conviction that rape is an extremely common crime. It is not. My guess is that not one out of every thousand women who read this book will ever be raped. Though the rate is increasing, the most recent FBI statistics show that even in our largest cities, where the rape rate is highest, only 85 out of every 100,000 women will be raped each year. Of course, even a single rape victim is one too many, but I want you to know that rape isn't inevitable, far from it. And, says the FBI, if you live in a town of 10,000 or less, your chances of being raped are only a fifth as great as if you live in a large metropolitan area. I disagree with the FBI here, though it doesn't change the point. My figures show the per capita rape rate is about equal between large city and small town.

For many women, the fear of rape has racial overtones, yet the National Commission on Crime found that 90 percent of the time the rapist and his victim are of the same race. My research also shows that this is true in 94 percent of these cases. Not only are rapists and victims usually of the same race, they almost always live in the same neighborhood. Amir, in his study of Philadelphia rape cases, found that rapist and victim lived in the same neighborhood 82 percent of the time. D. A. Eralson, who studied 2,624 sex crimes in Chicago, came up with exactly the same figure.

I don't ask you to memorize all these numbers, but the point they make is worth remembering: rape isn't as common as the popular mythology insists and it isn't necessarily as dangerous as the news would have you believe. Sure, it's something to fear. It's a danger to recognize. But if you become obsessed with rape, it's self-defeating.

Unfortunately, there are some people who take rape *too* lightly. Most men, for instance. Some clods even claim there isn't any such thing as rape. They say that no woman can be raped unless she cooperates. You hear that in the locker room, the bar room and, I'm sorry to say, you hear it in the courtroom. It's usually put this way: one woman can't be raped by one man.

De Gramont's mother advised him, as part of his sexual education, that there was no such thing as rape. "All a girl has to do is cross her legs," she said, "and if she has to fight off a man, he will get so flustered that he won't be able to do anything."

"I have since discovered," writes de Gramont, "that she was wrong on both counts: that fear makes women submit to force and that the rapist, far from being flustered, is sometimes a man who can only perform in a struggle."

Amir puts it more scientifically in his book: "A statement was made to the effect that a woman can resist rape 'because of the almost inexpugnable position she occupies on account of the topography of the sexual organs of the female body . . .'" (Which is nothing more than a fancy way of saying she can always cross her legs.)

"On the other hand," Amir writes, "various conditions, psychological and social in nature, may make rape possible. Among these are: the disproportion in physical strength between victim and attacker; the victim's being in an unconscious condition . . . ; the element of surprise which overcomes or neutralizes victim resistance; a threat which paralyzes or subdues initial resistance by the victim; fatalistic feeling and fear of bodily harm from blows and beating . . ."

That's nothing more than common sense, right? Yet nearly every day, in some courtroom somewhere in the United States, a defense attorney stands in front of the jury waving a Coke bottle around while his assistant vainly tries to stick a pencil into it—proof positive that rape is impossible. If I could, I'd like to add one more actor to that little drama: a good Samaritan who knocks that attorney unconscious or ties him up so that he can't move, or stomps on his arm until it's limp or simply puts a knife to his throat or a gun to his head. Then the prosecutor could spend an hour or two playing stick the pencil in the Coke bottle, until everyone sees how simple it is, including the defense attorney and the jury.

As Hunter S. Thompson wrote, in *Hell's Angels,* "Any lawyer who says there's no such thing as rape should be hauled out to a public place by three large perverts and buggered at high noon, with all his clients watching." I don't like the word "pervert" but I agree with his sentiment entirely.

Another, much larger group of people, while they freely admit that rape is possible, are convinced that the victim and her assaulter *share* the responsibility for the act. Even the rape victim herself may have moments of uncertainty here.

Menachem Amir has written that 75 percent of all rapes are "victim-precipitated"—that is, three-quarters of the time a woman brings about her own rape, at least in part. That's wrong. In one sense, in terms of the rapist's perception, 100 percent of the women who are raped encourage it, but about 99 percent of them aren't aware they're being perceived as encouraging rape and don't mean to be.

I'm talking now about teasing, sexually stimulating behavior. Folklore has it that women who tease get raped. It would follow, then, that if you don't want to be raped, you shouldn't tease. But that's easier said than done. Teasing, like beauty, is in the eye of the beholder. Women can, and do tease when they want to, but their behavior is sometimes interpreted as teasing when nothing could be further from their minds. You tease simply by being female. In other words, the responsibility for teasing in our society is laid on women, even when the woman isn't teasing but it is the man who perceives she's teasing. In our society, like it or not, men see women as sex objects. Some men go beyond this, but few—at least few heterosexual men—can entirely reverse a lifetime of training and eliminate all thoughts of sex when they see a woman. So the only way you can be sure you never tease is to stay in hiding twenty-four hours a day, three hundred and sixty-five days a year, from birth to death. And even then some men would firmly believe you're just being coy—playing "hard to get"—and would break in.

A woman must assume she's teasing some man on some occasion, no matter what she does. In other words, everyone is not on her wavelength. Let's say that a girl sitting in a restaurant or on a beach smiles at a boy sitting a few seats away. Maybe she means this as nothing more than a smile, friendly but impersonal. Maybe he's been staring at her and her smile is merely a nervous reaction to his steady gaze. Some men will accept her smile as just that, a smile. Another will take it as a come-on signifying anything—or everything. And later, when he ends up raping her, he'll say, in a surprised, self-righteous tone of voice, "Well, she teased me. She was asking for it."

These male attitudes are augmented and more readily expressed when a woman shows any desire for companionship. Ask any woman who has gone to a singles' bar, or has invited a man to her apartment, or has gone to his. "She knew what to expect," or, "Why else did she come here?" is the common male reaction and often the excuse for sexual aggressiveness.

He's not lying, necessarily. That may be how he saw it. The problem here is one of *perception* and *communication*. A man may receive what he thinks is an obvious invitation from a woman who is broadcasting nothing in particular. Then, he acts on what he thinks she's conveying, ignoring her thoughts on the subject, forgetting to treat her as a fellow human being, an *equal* participant in life.

A lot of people think that when a woman is wearing a miniskirt, a bikini or hot pants, she's teasing. I say that a woman doesn't have to wear a swimsuit to tease. She's teasing even when she wears a snowsuit. That's the reason, by the way, that I don't think today's skimpy fashions have anything to do with the rising rape rate. And Dr. Morris A. Lipton, chairman of the psychiatry department at the University of North Carolina's medical school, agrees with me. "All women's fashions—their attire, their perfumes, their hairdos—have always been designed to impart sexual attraction," he says, "but I think the miniskirt is no more significant a stimulus to rape than a tight sweater was twenty years ago or a spiked heel was ten years ago."

It's not how a woman dresses, it's what the man perceives she means by her outfit. Some men, when they see a bra-less coed, or a woman wearing a halter top and hot pants, feel there's a message here and the message is "Take me!" The message may actually be "I like to stay in fashion," or "I think I look nice wearing these clothes," or "I'm comfortable in this outfit," or even "Eat your heart out, Buster." But that doesn't matter. Some men would see a "Take me!" message even if you were wearing a tent. We shouldn't blame women for the weaknesses of men, but we do.

There are many other ways you can broadcast signals you don't intend. Your walk can do it, the way you carry yourself, or the way you sit, or the way you stand, or your air. Some men may perceive your air of confidence or even your air of shyness as teasing. That isn't the way it should be, but that's the way it is.

I'm making two points here: first, you can't avoid teasing; second, unless you're a mind reader, there's no way you can know for sure what it is about you that a man may perceive as teasing.

Incidentally, I think a woman has the right to act any way she wants to, even if that includes conscious teasing, without being raped as a result. You have the right to dress the way you want to, without feeling that in one outfit or another, men will think you're easy. You have the right to go where you want to and do what you want to without being the brunt of Victorian prejudices. You have the right to be treated as a human being. Your behavior and attire are your choice, and neither one—no matter how it might arouse or offend—justifies rape. Nothing does. In other words, I am saying that *never* is it the woman's fault in rape. Nothing she does ever gives a man the right to divorce himself from the human race and become an animal. But I do say that you should be aware that how you look and where you go and how you act has an effect on the men with whom you come into contact. The men you see on the street are not like your boyfriend or husband. They don't know you.

To do him proper justice, Menachem Amir wasn't referring only to teasing when he said that 75 percent of the rapes he studied were victim-precipitated. He and a number of other professionals—psychiatrists, psychologists and sociologists (and not all of them men)—think that many women have a hand in their own rapes because they harbor an unconscious desire for just that. These women, or so the theory goes, frequent places where the odds of rape are high, or they seek out certain types of men, then send out unconscious signals that encourage the assault. Just why do women do this? According to those who hold the theory, women behave this way either because they have a masochistic streak and they want to punish themselves for some misdeed or because rape relieves them of the responsibility (and perhaps the guilt) of having sexual relations by their own choice. You may not think much of this theory, and to tell you the truth, it doesn't exactly thrill me either. On the other hand, the psychological literature describes what's said to be a fairly common female fantasy that women might mistake for an unconscious desire to be raped. Apparently, many women have daydreamed at one time or another of being dragged into the bushes by, say, Paul Newman or Robert Redford and subjected to mad, passionate love. So when the subject or the actual event of rape comes up, these women are vulnerable to suggestions that they might somehow have unconsciously encouraged the assault.

I'd like to knock down that notion right now. Being dragged into the bushes to make love to a man who triples your heartbeat when you do no more than just think about him is not the same as being raped by a man you didn't choose, under the threat of death or severe bodily harm. In my opinion, the Paul Newman daydream isn't a rape fantasy at all, since it lacks the element that turns sexual intercourse into rape—genuine unwillingness. This fantasy, I think, is really a romantic one, a half-wish to be swept off your feet, not the expression of an unconscious desire to be raped.

There are a few women, I suppose, who *do* unconsciously desire rape, and in one way or another, encourage it, perhaps by leading a man past what they know is his point of no return, or by frequenting certain kinds of parties or certain neighborhoods where the risk of rape is higher than normal. Frankly, in the ten years I've been lecturing on rape prevention, I've never come across a woman who meets that description. I've met women who were fond of teasing, I've met women who sought romance, I've met women who liked to flirt—plenty of them. But I've never come across one who appeared to want to be raped.

The other part of the psychological theory, that some women seek rape because it's a way to have sexual inter-course without taking any responsibility for it, can't be dismissed so easily. I don't believe for a moment that women get themselves raped by strangers for this reason. But it may play a part in rape by someone you know— your date, for example.

Most women who are dragged into the bushes by a stranger and sexually assaulted have no trouble whatever deciding whether or not they wanted to have sexual inter-course with the guy. For the woman who has sexual inter-course with her date, however, there may be grounds for confusion. Sometimes there is a mighty fine line between seduction and rape. The woman may be unwilling immedi-ately before intercourse and, again, immediately afterward. But only she can know for sure whether or not she was unwilling during the act. Given all the subtle and not-so-subtle means of persuasion a persistent man has at his com-mand, and given the fact that you may not only be strug-gling to say no to the man but also to yourself, you may have a hard time deciding whether or not it was really rape. You may want to salve your conscience by telling yourself that it was.

In the last analysis, only the woman knows if she's been raped, and then only if she's a woman who knows her own mind. It is possible that her boyfriend won't know, since he's probably been taught from birth that all women say, "No, no, we mustn't," and that such objections are just part of the game. The average man has a tough time telling the difference between a woman who is mouthing the words her mother taught her and the woman who really doesn't want to have sex. And he'll be inclined to think her objections aren't heartfelt, since his own desires are involved. Even if they have sexual intercourse only after a struggle, the man may think he's only acting as his date expects him to, since in our society men are taught that women like it when the man is physically forceful during sex. Regardless of the truth.

There is one other circumstance where women might logically be considered at least partly responsible for their own rape: when they are assaulted by a man who didn't start out with rape in mind. Although it is rare, women unwittingly can and do turn simple purse-snatchings, robberies, muggings or burglaries into rape. By the way they react when approached by an assaulter, they can transform him from a frightened rabbit, ready to run, into a tiger bent on rape and maybe more. But even here, I hold that it isn't the woman who is responsible for the rape.

The question of responsibility often comes up during my lectures, in a subtle way. Usually, it happens like this: during the question period, someone stands up and asks me what sort of women are most likely to get raped. I know she's looking for an answer that will exclude women of *her* type, whatever that is. I wish I could answer her the way she wants.

The fact is, *any* kind of woman is a potential rape victim: pretty women, ugly women, smart women, stupid women, fat women, slender women, young women, old women, white women, black women, virgins, prostitutes, nuns in their habits, nurses in uniform, little old ladies in tennis shoes, little girls in sneakers, policewomen, schoolteachers, ministers' wives, college women, high school girls, grade school girls, women who work in factories, women who clip coupons, sensitive women, callous women, movie stars, housewives, popular girls, wallflowers, rich women, poor women—*you*, if you're a woman. The Sex Crimes Analysis Unit of the New York City Police Department has received reports of rapes of females from three months to eighty-six years old.

Character, socioeconomic status, dating habits, place of residence, occupation, appearance and age, no matter what they are, do not exempt a woman from rape. Oh, there are some risk factor variations from group to group, but they're just statistics, meaningless in individual instances.

2

The Creature from the Black Lagoon

Why do men rape? For that matter, why don't women rape?

Well, to answer the second question first, women *do* rape, sometimes. Every once in a while, you read a newspaper story about a gang of vicious women who've waylaid some unfortunate fellow and sexually assaulted him. But up to now, at least, rape by females in our society has been so rare that most men consider it a joking matter. They say, "If only it would happen to me." If it did, they might not be so flippant about it, since in the few recorded instances in this country of rape by women, their victims have not only been sexually assaulted, but also severely mutilated.

Though rape by women certainly isn't customary in the United States, the reverse is true in some other societies. The Colombian anthropologist G. Reichel-Dolmatoff, in his description of the Kogi, a tribe of the Sierra Nevada de Santa Marta in Colombia, says that women of this tribe often band together in twos or threes, ambush the men of their tribe on roads or fields, and violate them sexually. Bronislaw Malinowski, the famous Polish anthropologist, in his book *The Sexual Life of Savages in Northwestern Melanesia*, tells of orgiastic assaults on men by women of the village of Vakuta and several other nearby villages. And there are other examples of this in other, little-known societies.

I'm not just trying to entertain you with what seem to be tidbits from Ripley's *Believe It or Not*. The fact that women are the rapists in some societies, however few, strongly suggests that the *character of the society* has at least something to do with which sex does the raping. And for that matter, how prevalent rape is.

That leads me back to Question one: Why do men rape? Or, to put it a bit differently now, what is it about our society that leads men to be rapists? If I could cite a single responsible factor, I'd say that rape was a by-product of the overall pressure our competitive society puts on its male contingent, giving men the impression that all things in life are there for the taking. This attitude is now so ingrained in our social structure that it's taught to both sexes, from birth on. The result is conditioned behavior that reaches into the very core of human familial relationships and the roles men and women play in society. Men tend to be overtly aggressive on the whole and most of the forces of society encourage this in one way or another. Women, by and large, tend to be overtly passive and are likewise encouraged to act this way. There are exceptions, of course, but I'm talking about the broad, overall picture. In other words, our society, though it is slowly changing, perpetuates the myth that men are the providers, women the provided-for; men are the requesters, women the accepters or rejecters; men take the initiative sexually, women respond.

The result of this arrangement is a sort of discrimination against both sexes. Given prevailing social attitudes, it's unacceptable for men to be passive, or for women to be aggressive. Whatever other effect these attitudes may have, then, there's no question that they limit the individual freedom of choice each human being is or should be entitled to. Although these standards are changing, it will take a long time for society to eliminate them.

In the long run, if the conditions that make rape possible in our society are to be eliminated, some of our prevailing attitudes on the roles of the sexes must change.

It is this aggressive role that men play in our society that makes rapists out of some of them, I believe. Among the psychologists and psychiatrists who have studied the subject, there are a dozen or so theories on why a man rapes, most of them fairly similar.

My own analysis may sound oversympathetic toward rapists, but it's not. It is, instead, an attempt to understand their motivation in order to prevent rape. If I seem to view rapists as no more than human beings with troubles, I do so with the sole purpose of understanding and preventing rape. If I ask you to view them the same way, it's for the same reason. Neither of us is "soft on rapists."

I believe there are two types of rapists. There is a very large group of men who put women on a pedestal for one reason or another. Usually, these men start out in childhood overidealizing their mothers, seeing them as pure, kind, forgiving, beautiful. This image is so strong for some men that, by contrast, they see themselves as inadequate or inferior.

Most of the time, these feelings of inadequacy or inferiority fade, overcome by a loving mother–son relationship. But not always. Some men are really rejected by their mothers or by other women important in their lives or else they perceive that they are rejected. Their feelings of inferiority solidify instead of dissolving. They begin to over-idealize all women.

Some of these men will eventually have successful relationships with women and their ill opinion of themselves will change enough so that they can function perhaps quite well. Others will have repeated failures, confirming their feelings of inferiority.

Now, to a certain degree, all men are diffident toward women (I'm using "diffident" as the exact opposite of "confident"). That's because men incessantly receive male peer-group pressure as well as overall societal pressure to make initial social contact with members of the opposite sex. To do this, a man must bare his ego—strip himself of his defenses. Meanwhile the woman is in the enviable position of accepting or rejecting. Some rejections are inevitable, and few men are so self-confident that rejection doesn't hurt. Thus the stage is set for a defeatist attitude that most men would find difficult to surmount. In an immature man, this eventually feeds the fires of inferiority and persecution. Imagine, for example, how an eighth-grader feels at the class dance when he bravely crosses the floor to ask a girl to dance, only to get turned down.

The man who starts out thinking that women are worthy of worship and that he is a lowly creature indeed is diffident in the extreme. And yet, our society tells all men, even those who are mired in feelings of inadequacy, that they must be aggressive, that they must take the initiative with women; otherwise, they won't be "acting like men." To preserve what's left of his self-image, the man who feels inadequate is likely to try again and again to win some woman's esteem. Most times, his attempts are doomed before they start. Burdened by his feelings of inadequacy and his awe of women, such a man's efforts to gain affection are almost certain to be awkward and inept. Usually, at the first sign of real resistance on the part of the woman, a man like this will fold up and crawl away, his ego shattered like a light bulb dropped on the sidewalk. With every rejection he becomes more and more diffident, more and more socially inept. Eventually he may be totally unable to approach a woman in the accepted manner. He may be too frightened.

Now, the man has what the behavioral psychologists call an "approach-avoidance" conflict. He desperately wants the love of a woman. And society says he should ask for it—and be able to get it. Yet he knows from experience that if he makes the attempt, he'll wind up hurt and humiliated.

No one likes to feel afraid and inadequate. When such feelings gets strong enough, when they hurt too much, the mind denies them. It then falls back on its defenses— rationalization, compensation, repression, regression or displacement, singly or in combination. In high-stress situations, the defenses can crack. The result is frustration, then hostility. This hostility is often directed at the original problem—women, all women.

A lot of men get into this position. Maybe both men and women feel this way one time or another, but for most of us the anger subsides after a while. Those women who remain angry at men rarely act on their feelings, probably in part because that lies outside society's view of how women should act. And most of the men who harbor such anger toward women likewise keep it bottled up.

One group doesn't. They rape. Their anger drives them to act aggressively toward women, humiliating them, defiling them, beating them, having sexual intercourse with them against their will, symbolically dragging them down from their pedestal—even though the pedestal exists only in the mind of the man who's doing the dragging. By bringing women down, they are, in effect, *raising themselves up*.

For these men, rape is a way to pay back the pain women have caused them, and therefore a way to vanquish their feelings of inferiority and inadequacy. For such men, rape is the means to defile and humiliate the woman. Such rape is motivated not by passion, but by hate.

Another aspect of this type of motivation goes back to the rapist's relation with his mother. The anger and resentment he may have felt toward her is now played out on his victims whom he sees as the surrogate for that most significant woman in his life.

These men are emotionally unstable. I don't mean that they are raving maniacs. They are emotionally disturbed, maladjusted. In particular high-stress situations they are unable to keep their actions within the normal social limitations in at least one area—male–female relationships. The rapist may seem normal in every way—except in his tendency to rape. He may be capable of thinking his way through a very complex situation, like the assault itself, taking into account every possible factor—opportunity, time of day, how often an area is patrolled, lighting conditions, privacy. He may be able to laugh at someone's jokes, feel sad at the news of a tragedy, do anything else any other person can do, *except* stay within society's limits when it comes to male–female relations. And he may even be able to do that most of the time.

What I'm saying—and it is the single most important statement in this book—is that the rapist is a human being, a person, someone you could relate to under other circumstances. He is someone you can *communicate* with like any other person in any circumstance—including rape.

On the surface there's nothing inhuman about what the rapist wants from you. He wants three things: sexual fulfillment sometimes, female companionship a lot of the time, and most of the time what the psychologists call "ego enhancement," the good feelings about himself.

It's easy enough to see how the rapist can get sexual fulfillment. And even the pleasure of companionship is obvious enough. But you might well ask, just how can the act of rape give a man good feelings about himself? The answer lies in the nature of ego enhancement. Everyone— you, I, your boyfriend, the man who rapes—needs and wants ego enhancement. We all want to feel good about ourselves. We would all like to feel stronger, smarter, better-looking, more needed, more respected, more of a person. There are two ways to go about getting ego enhancement. The first is to feel that you've achieved something positive. It's this impulse that's behind most of humanity's accomplishments. The second is to raise yourself up by stepping on someone else either directly or indirectly. This impulse is responsible for many of the bad things in the world, from murder to arson to child-beating to prejudice—to rape.

The man who rapes is trying to feel good about himself at the woman's expense. He wants to feel that he's as good as he thinks she is. He puts women on a pedestal, you'll recall. To knock his victim down to his level, he believes he must humiliate her, he must dirty her, he must show her "who's boss." He must establish dominance, reversing his lifetime pattern with women, and the simplest, most obvious, most spectacular way to do this in most cases is to have sexual intercourse with her against her will.

If his assault succeeds in giving him the ego enhancement he desires, he's reinforced and he'll rape again and again, in the same way that if you go to the movies and have a good time you'll probably go to the movies again.

This analysis does not include the second type of rapist, the type who might be called the "100 percent pure sexist rapist." This is the man who actually thinks women are "asking for it," that they "want it," whatever they say, however they act. On a date, he's the man who believes that when a woman goes partway willingly, she's demonstrating that she wants to have sexual intercourse. So he makes sure that she gets what she wants. Or, in the same situation, he's the man who believes that if a woman goes partway, she's teasing and she owes him the rest.

This man, when he sees a woman hitchhiking, assumes she wants to have sex. He believes that when a woman—any woman—goes certain places, wears certain clothing, walks a certain way, looks a certain way, talks a certain way, befriends certain people, she is really "asking for it."

Yet, psychologist Ralph Garofalo and his colleagues at the Center for Diagnosis and Treatment of Sexually Dangerous Persons in Bridgewater, Massachusetts, after extensive personality tests and interviews with more than a hundred rapists, have, among other conclusions, pointed out that, on balance, the rapist is not an exotic freak. In some cases his behavior is merely an extreme manifestation of the normal male sex drive. The crucial distinction, Garofalo explains, is that normal men find a socially acceptable outlet for their desires, while the rapist loses all sight of moral or legal considerations. "In many cases," he observes, "these guys end up feeling really sorry. They realize they were dealing with an overwhelming impulse." I couldn't agree more.

Is there a way that you can tell a man is a rapist just by looking at him, or by talking with him? Do such men send out signals or give discernible clues to their mental states?

Well, I've studied more than four thousand rape cases, and so far as physical appearance, occupation and apparent mastery of the social graces go, I've been unable to construct a profile of the rapist. As for appearance, he looks like anyone else; he may be Ivy League or hippie, young or old, good-looking or not-so-good-looking, tall or short, fat or thin, white, black, yellow, red or any combination. In personality, too, he may be awkward or glib, nasty or charming, friendly or hostile. In short, the characteristics of the rapist are as varied as those of his victim. He is, after all, a human being. He looks like a human being, acts like a human being and talks like a human being. In fact, the only important difference between the rapist and his fellow human beings is that he does something they don't do. He rapes.

Contrary to popular opinion, most of the time rapists and their victims aren't even strangers. Over the years, I've found that in about 35 percent of the rape cases the woman was assaulted by her own date, in the dating environment. Very few rapes of this type are reported. Most women (or men) have an emotional stake of their own in portraying their dates as acceptable, even desirable, human beings. About 35 percent of the time the rapist is someone else you know—a friend, neighbor, boss, co-worker, relative, friend of a friend—in other words, someone you thought you could trust, someone you never dreamed presented any sort of a threat to you. Rape in these cases often goes unreported, too, for a variety of reasons, including the embarrassment of innocent parties, perhaps those through whom you know the rapist. Finally, about 30 percent of the time the rapist will be a total stranger, someone the woman didn't know at all, though he may have known who she was or seen her several times prior to the attack. More rapes of this type are reported to the police than of any other kind.

A number of times men have approached me after my lecture on rape prevention and admitted to me that they were rapists, or that they had a tremendous desire to rape and were afraid they'd lose control. The first time it happened was at a small college in Ohio, in 1966. I'd just finished talking to an audience of several hundred when a big fellow came up to me and drew me aside. There wasn't anything particularly unusual about him, except, perhaps, that he wore his hair very short and he wasn't dressed in the free style of the day. Other than that, he was a nice-looking guy with a pleasant, sincere manner.

"Mr. Storaska," he said, "I'm one of those fellows you were talking about."

"What?"

"I have that need. To rape, I mean. I haven't done it yet, but I want to—and I know I shouldn't."

I don't know if you can imagine how shocked I was. I was quite accustomed to talking with a group of women after each lecture, each of them telling me in detail of an experience she or a friend had had. But now I was about to hear it from the other side, and from the way this man was talking, I wasn't at all sure he was telling the truth about not having raped yet.

"Girls make me so angry," he told me. "They're always laughing at me. Even when I'm just walking down the street, they're laughing at me and putting me down. When they do that, I want to bash in their goddamn heads."

I particularly remember the power and anger in that last remark. People nearby turned toward us when they heard the force of it. He pulled me away a few steps and went on.

"I just don't know what's the matter with me," he said. "Even when I open a door for a girl, she never thanks me. It's like I got some kind of disease." For a moment I paused to suggest some ways that he could get some psychological assistance. But he was edgy already, and I didn't want anything to break the bond between us. It was a kind of minor miracle that he was confiding in me the way he was. I tried to help him as best I could.

"You know," I said, "when I walk down the street and see a woman laughing or smiling in my direction, I don't think she's laughing at me, I think she's flirting with me.

You know something, the girl you saw laughing at you could have been flirting with you. And the one I saw could have been putting me down. It all depends on the way you perceive things. And how you perceive depends in great part on what's happened to you before and how you perceived that."

He was listening to me and I seemed to be getting through.

"If I were you," I said, choosing my words very carefully now, "I'd dress as sharp as I could, because you can never look too good. Then when a woman laughed or smiled at me, I'd smile back. You're a good-looking fellow. More times than not, I'll bet you'll find the women are smiling because they're attracted to you or at least want to be friends."

He gave me a puzzled look, almost as if the thought hadn't ever occurred to him quite that way.

"If I were you," I went on, "I'd stop in and talk with my guidance counselor about it. If you prefer, I'll even go with you—to break the ice. I've yet to meet one who didn't sincerely try to understand and help."

But as I was talking I knew the answer already. He, like so many women who had already come to me at the end of my lecture, came for three reasons: (1) he knew I was going to be empathetic about any problem he had; (2) he needed desperately to talk to someone; (3) he knew he probably wouldn't have to face me again.

By this time, others were pushing toward me through the crowd and our moment of privacy was fast coming to an end.

"Maybe," he said. "I'll think about that."

He drifted away as a pair of coeds approached me. I never saw or heard from him again.

Recently another rapist talked to me after a lecture in Pennsylvania. This fellow was about nineteen, had medium-length blond hair and was nicely dressed. I think the aver-age woman would have found him decidedly attactive. And that isn't so surprising. Many women have described their assaulters to me in exactly those terms. Many have even said that in another circumstance they would have dated the guy. In fact, I do know of one case where a woman ended up *marrying* a man who tried to assault her, a complete stranger at the time of the assault.

The man at the Pennsylvania lecture looked no different from the guy you dated last night, or a shoe salesman, or an English instructor, or the mechanic who fixed your flat. He wasn't a four-armed Martian or a raving maniac who materialized only when the moon was full.

"You weren't putting rapists down in your lecture," he started out. "You were treating them as people. I can't tell you how good that made me feel. Because I've raped."

I managed to keep my composure and led him away from the podium so that I could talk to him in private as long as possible. I wanted to help him if I could, and I wanted to learn from him.

"I guess I've raped about a dozen girls," he said. "And I don't know if I will rape again. I just can't help it when it happens. I know it's wrong and I want to stop, but I don't know how."

As I had advised the man in Ohio to seek help, so I advised this young man, though I knew it was probably futile. "The best thing you can do is try to find out more about yourself," I said. "That's awfully hard to do by your-self. A guidance counselor or a psychologist or even a close friend would help. And the fact that you've come to me is the best indication that you want to get hold of yourself and understand your problem."

We managed to talk for several minutes. Like the other rapist I had talked to, this man seemed ready to bolt. For him, just talking about himself this honestly was an enormously courageous act. I thought briefly of trying to contact the school authorities or even the police, but I realized how easy it would be for him to deny he'd ever made any admissions to me or to say the whole thing was a practical joke. In fact, the possibility crossed my mind that he was joking. But from his tone of voice and his intense concern, I knew that he wasn't. I decided to talk with him as long as I could and learn as much as possible.

"Does something trigger you into the act?" I asked.

He thought a moment. "I date a normal amount," he said. "And usually nothing happens. But when a girl tries to shoot me down, when she tries to belittle me, it makes me so angry I want to rip her apart. That's when it happens. When they're nice to me, it takes all my anger away. I just want to be treated as a person. Is that too much to ask?"

Evidently someone in his past had felt that it was too much to ask, or at least that had been his perception. Before the conversation ended, he'd agreed to see a counselor. Whether or not he actually did, I never knew. He never contacted me after that, although I encouraged him to. I never even found out his name, since I was certain that if I had asked for it he would have been frightened off.

These aren't the only rapists I've talked to. I've talked to dozens of others, in police stations, in campus security offices, or in jails, as well as in the situations described above. If these men have one thing in common, it's that they're not monsters. Rapists are people, people with a problem—a problem that you can either fuel or help extinguish by your attitude.

3

Conventional Wisdom
—and
Conventional Stupidity

Advice on what to do to save yourself from rape is easy to come by these days. Magazine and newspaper articles, police department pamphlets and self-defense books for women abound.

In most of them, women are told to scream as loud as they can, for as long as they can, in the event of an assault. They're told to struggle with all their might. They're told to run, and if that's not possible, to cry or plead or faint, or if necessary, surrender totally ("relax and enjoy it," as if such a thing were possible).

They're also told to study self-defense. They're told to learn karate, kung fu, judo or jujitsu, or aikido, or if that's too much trouble, they're advised to learn how to cripple a man with a stomp on his instep, double him over with a punch in the solar plexus, leave him squirming in pain with a kick in the groin, or skewer him with an umbrella.

Or they're told to carry weapons in their purses at all times: tear gas pens or Mace, fingernail files, rattail combs, hatpins, knives, revolvers and the like. Or they're told to attempt to knock their assaulter senseless by bashing him over the head with a book or a purse.

All of this advice fits neatly into one category, the one marked *worthless*. Except in one rare circumstance, when a woman finds herself in *immediate* danger of her life or severe bodily harm, *not one* of these tactics is the right thing to do if you're assaulted. And I don't care where you got the advice—from your local police chief, your husband, your mother, your father, your brother on the football team, a self-defense instructor, or the president of your local women's group. It's wrong, and I intend to prove that to you.

Each and every one of these tactics violates one or more of the three basic, common-sense laws of assault safety.

The first law is *Don't antagonize*. The rapist, you'll remember, is an angry, emotionally disturbed person. Now, what happens when you antagonize a person who isn't emotionally disturbed, someone who isn't angry to begin with, by screaming, fighting, hitting or using weapons against him? Well, he *becomes* angry. Imagine what happens when you do the same thing to a man who's already in an unstable condition—or is given to instability, in this area anyway. Chances are very good that he'll explode. All over you.

The second law is *Don't commit your behavior*. To put it another way, make sure that anything you do is reversible. If you try to kick your assaulter in the groin and miss, or bop him over the head with a book and it turns out he's got a noggin made out of granite, what do you say? "I just wanted to call your attention to this new best seller"? By your actions, you have once and for all established the ground rules for the confrontation. If you've struggled, screamed, kicked, used weapons or practiced your judo or karate on the rapist, those ground rules start with *violence* and there is no turning back. The winner then is a matter of chance—or of who is better at violent action—and chance is what I'm trying to eliminate.

By the way, fainting also commits your behavior. When you faint, you are from that moment on totally defenseless. If your assaulter decides to murder you, you'll never even be able to offer a dissenting opinion.

The third law is *Do nothing that can hurt you.* In other words, whatever you do, make sure that either it will work all the time, or if it happens not to work, at least it won't make things worse. And *any* kind of antagonistic behavior, from fighting to cursing to making a nasty face, or having him think you are fighting or cursing or making a nasty face can make things worse.

I will be the first to admit that when you scream or struggle or cry or beg or do anything else that could be perceived by the assaulter as being antagonistic or violent he will just turn and run, lacking the courage to follow through with the assault, about 50 percent of the time. *But what about the other 50 percent?* That's when he smashes you with his fist, cuts you up with a knife, maims you, rapes you, kills you.

I refuse to advocate any method of rape prevention that could cause the bodily harm or death of *any* person using it. That's why I believe all of the antagonistic techniques mentioned above are the wrong thing to do in the event of an assault.

Let's start with *screaming.* Except, possibly, in a single unusual circumstance, I *do not* advocate that a woman scream if she is assaulted. Whenever I say that during a lecture, someone always asks, "But won't someone hear you if you scream?" Very possibly someone will. But what then? Some years ago in New York City, a woman named Kitty Genovese was attacked in the courtyard of an apartment building. She screamed her lungs out and some forty-four people heard her. Not one of them even called the police. Her attacker dawdled over her, finally knifing her to death while everyone watched. I wish I could tell you this case was an exception, but time after time, women scream while being assaulted, people hear them—and do nothing. Something just as bad happened in an Oregon college dorm a few years ago, so such things are not limited to New York or other large metropolitan areas.

Does the rapist want to hear you scream? No, he doesn't. Will he try to stop you? Yes, he will. Will he hold his finger up to his lips and say, "Ssshhh!"? Not likely. He'll try to stop you any way he can. And the louder and longer you scream, the harder he'll try to stop you.

In one case I know of, a woman screamed when she was attacked, and when her assaulter started beating her up in an effort to turn off the screams, she kept yelling. After a while, he started stuffing things into her mouth. Still she screamed. Then he began to choke her. She finally went limp, just before she lost consciousness. Her assaulter stopped choking her and took out what he'd jammed into her mouth. It seems to me that the assaulter was giving his victim a message all along. The message was "Shut up!" She took an awfully long time to comprehend it. If she'd taken any longer she might not have survived the attack. This is not to say she was behaving badly and the rapist reasonably. In such a situation it's a question of the woman deciding on a course of action which will give her the best chance to survive a violent encounter with someone who is emotionally disturbed.

Still, if this rapist's reaction to screaming sounds like the reaction of a raving maniac or a mad dog, I ask you to consider what *you* would do to an innocent little device known as an alarm clock if, one morning, pushing the button on the back didn't turn it off. You'd hit it, you'd stomp on it, you'd fling it against a wall, you'd smash it with a shoe, you'd throw it out the window if necessary—anything to stop the damn ringing, right? And, I assume, you're an emotionally stable person, unlike the rapist. To the rapist, I'd guess that a woman screaming is like a thousand alarm clocks going off simultaneously. If the noise doesn't scare him away—and you won't know in advance who scares and who doesn't—the only thing that he'll be able to think about is, "How can I stop that noise?" In the end, he'll do anything to turn off his alarm clock.

I said that there was one unusual circumstance in which I might advocate screaming. This is it: if you can be a hundred percent sure that help is actually within hearing distance of your screams, a hundred percent sure that the help *will* respond, a hundred percent sure that the help will be *entirely adequate* to meet the situation, and a hundred percent sure that the assaulter—either with a weapon or with his bare hands—won't do away with you *before* help arrives.

I can't imagine such a circumstance. Even if you're sitting in your own living room and you know your husband is upstairs reading a newspaper you shouldn't necessarily scream if you are attacked. Sure, your husband will hear you and respond, but will he be able to handle your assaulter? And can you be certain the intruder won't turn out to have a knife, or get so angry at your screams that he throttles you? I think not.

Even if you're out in a car someplace and your date or some stranger or group of strangers attacks you and you see a regiment of policemen walking by, not ten feet away, you can't be *sure* you won't be dead by the time help arrives. After all, the assaulter wouldn't have much to lose by killing you, would he? As I say in my lectures, you shouldn't scream even if your house is surrounded by a hundred thousand marines and you're being attacked in your bedroom by a single man, because he could do more than enough damage to you before anyone could get inside to help you.

Besides, there are better things you can do, as you'll see. *Struggling*, the second most frequently recommended reaction to assault, isn't one of them, though. I can imagine only one situation in which struggling is the right response to an assault, *only* one: if you perceive that you are faced with *immediate defense of your life*. (And with the struggling, I would advocate screaming. In other words, screaming only becomes a "choice" if you have *no other* resources at all.) In other situations, though struggling *may* cause the rapist to flee, if it doesn't it will cause him to redouble his attack, with perhaps horrendous consequences. You should not take that gamble, especially when you'll have other, better tactics to use.

Struggling won't help you at all if you're assaulted. Your struggles may sexually arouse your assaulter and make it easier for him to penetrate you. Furthermore, usually when a woman struggles while she's being raped, her sexual organs become mutilated and torn. And this is in addition to the beating she must endure for him to get this far. Remember, he wants to stop the Coke bottle from moving, so struggling gains you nothing except rape *plus* mutilation.

It usually takes a man three to five *minutes* to become sufficiently sexually aroused to have sexual intercourse—when his partner is willing. If a woman struggles, the man's sexual arousal time is likely to drop to between five and ten *seconds*. Struggling enhances the pleasurable sexual sensations the rapist feels as he begins penetration. It also gives him a feeling of power, since he is subduing a protesting woman.

As Paul H. Gebbard and his colleagues at the Kinsey Institute for Sex Research point out in their book, *Sex Offenders*, many mammals engage in a struggle before sexual intercourse, ranging from extreme violence (as with the mink) to something akin to playful wrestling. "The physiological by-products of excitement and exertion," writes Gebhard, "the increased heart rate, increased breathing, muscle tension, the greater supply of blood to the body surfaces, etc.—all of these are also a part of sexual response and it is easy to see how these physiological conditions could facilitate sexual response."

So far, I've been talking about men who respond normally. Some rapists, perhaps most, fit into this category. But there are others who are impotent, who can't get an erection, unless their sexual partners are struggling. If you struggle with a rapist of this type, you're unwittingly doing him a favor.

You're not doing yourself a favor, though. You're asking for trouble. About a year before it vanished from the newsstands, *Life* magazine interviewed a number of muggers and assaulters. One of them said this: "If somebody hits me, watch out. One time, I threw this woman down, she started flailing and hit me in the face. I went haywire, really wild. I wanted to tear her apart, kill her. I caught myself in time, but I kept thinking, 'A broad hit me, a broad!'"

I have personal knowledge of a tragic case in which a young woman struggled while being assaulted. She was walking along at about one o'clock in the afternoon when a man came up to her from behind and put a knife to her throat. She hadn't heard my lecture, so she didn't know that she shouldn't scream and struggle. She did what she had read, or heard, or been conditioned to do: she tried to wriggle away. Either the man accidentally stabbed her or she accidentally moved into the blade of the knife. At any rate, she suffered a minor throat wound, just enough to draw blood. The sight of the blood, and the pain, perhaps, drove her berserk; she threw herself on the ground, struggling, screaming, hitting and kicking. Her assaulter just reached over and stabbed her in the throat. She was dead before help could arrive. This case was reconstructed by the town chief of police, the investigating agent of the state bureau of investigation and myself.

Why do women struggle? After a lecture in Denver a few years ago, a middle-aged woman told me, "They usually kill you anyhow, so what do you have to lose—you might as well struggle." Even if she were right about how often murder accompanies rape (and she wasn't), her logic was cockeyed. It was like saying that since a lot of people get killed in car accidents, we all might as well aim for a telephone pole and step on the accelerator.

A woman who struggles when assaulted does so because she really doesn't want to be raped and doesn't know better, or because she believes struggling is her best defense, or because she feels the need to prove she didn't want to be raped—to preserve what some people call her "virtue." (Or, at least, to give evidence to herself and others that she did her best to preserve it.) If she's raped, she can always say, "But I struggled. Here are the black and blue marks and the stitches and the wounds to prove it." That's what she can say if she's still alive.

Society bears much of the blame here. Mothers and fathers, husbands or boyfriends, policemen or judges seem to require that women who get raped had better come away with battle scars. If they don't, the judgment will come down against *them*, not the rapist. And sadly, this sometimes happens even if they have scars. However important "virtue" may be, it seems to me that whoever puts it above life and limb is confusing priorities.

There's another reason a woman might struggle during an assault that makes at least some sense: by doing so, she hopes to halt further attacks. That's the "feminist reason." Many of these women feel, and some are saying, that "if enough of us fight and struggle and enough rapists get bloodied, they'll stop." I think not. Although I agree with their outraged sentiments, I think that the woman who reacts to an assault by saying, "Who the hell do you think you are? What gives you the right to touch me? Why should I sit back and let you violate me?" and simultaneously screams and struggles, is throwing gasoline on a fire. Rapists are angry people out to humiliate their victims. The woman who struggles against her attacker on the basis of her right to say what may happen to her own body may be in for the beating of her life. Or she may lose her life altogether.

As for whether or not rapists will curb their impulses if enough of them are beaten up, I don't think they will. That kind of thinking assumes, first of all, that it could be accomplished; second, that a sound thrashing will transform the rapist into an emotionally stable individual; and third, that a beaten rapist will tell his fellow assaulters what's happened to him. More important, this attitude assumes that, in a contest of physical strength, a woman can defeat her assaulter—a very shaky assumption.

Some women are probably eager for a struggle with a potential assaulter. "Just let me at him," they say, at least to themselves. They are apparently confident that they would win in any fight.

Let's just say, for the sake of argument, that you're a big woman—five feet ten inches tall, say, and a hundred and seventy pounds, that you're a black belt in karate and that you're being assaulted by a man who's five inches shorter than you are and forty pounds lighter. Wonderwoman vs. son of Don Knotts. Should you struggle? When you can crack his spine with a tap from the side of your hand?

You should struggle if (1) you can be absolutely sure that the man has no weapon; (2) you can be absolutely sure that you are at least as quick as he is and/or can fight as well as he; (3) that the surprise of the assault will not dissipate your ability to fight; and (4) you know, positively, that he has no friend near by.

Is there such a situation? Can you possibly determine whether or not a man has a weapon? If he's naked and it's broad daylight and he does a pirouette for you so you can see he's holding nothing behind him—maybe. But very few rapists are this obliging. Can you know for sure that he's alone? Well, if you're both in the middle of a ten-acre meadow devoid of trees and bushes and the light is good enough for you to see in all directions, perhaps.

All right, let's assume those conditions are met: you *know* the man is alone and you *know* he has no weapon. Now, is there any way in the world, without full-scale Olympic competition, that given the circumstances of the assault you can be absolutely sure you'll be able to overpower him? Remember, he may be tiny, but he could be a third-degree black belt in karate while you're only a first.

There is only one way to find out for sure: struggle while you're being assaulted. But remember, you may be betting your life on the outcome. There is no situation within the limits of my imagination where struggling is the right reaction when you're approached by a rapist. Except the one specific case—immediate defense of your life. There is no situation in which you can be certain to win and nothing less than certainty will do.

But what if a woman *knows* how to defend herself? The chances are, you've read or heard of at least one physical self-defense technique, something so simple that no one has to teach you how to use it, and you have it in the back of your mind that if you're ever attacked this is what you'll do. I'm referring now to the various blows and kicks aimed at a variety of vulnerable spots on a man's body.

To guarantee success, whichever one of these you choose must do one thing to the rapist: it must *incapacitate* him so that you'll have more than enough time to get away. Anything less than incapacitation—for example, just hurting him severely—is the same as struggling, and is likely to only infuriate him further, to your detriment. If your assaulter is incapacitated, though, it hardly matters whether or not he is infuriated. He won't be able to do anything about his rage. He won't be able to do anything but lie there out cold or in shock or writhing in pain.

All right, that's the test: Can you be sure your technique will incapacitate your attacker? Let's see if any of the kicks and blows recommended for the assault situation meet that test.

Without a doubt, someone has told you at one time or another that you can always defend yourself against an assaulter with jabbing a *knee to his groin*, to his testicles, in fact. A well-placed knee to the testicles will send a man into shock, incapacitating him perhaps for hours. Men are extremely vulnerable in this area. Blows here can cause excruciating pain, and possibly even death—if only from shock alone.

Two factors render this method of self-defense just about worthless in the assault situation. First, there's the matter of height differences. If you're five foot two and your attacker is six foot three, how are you going to get your knee up there—ask him to stoop? And if you're taller than he is, do you ask him to stand on a box? When a man is standing or walking or running, or in almost any non-sexual situation, his penis is in front of his testicles, shielding them. Unlike the testicles, the penis is highly insensitive to pain. So it's the testicles you must reach, not just the general groin area.

What's more, in most positions, a man's thighs offer further protection for his testicles. If you do try to knee your attacker in the groin then, chances are very good that you'll fail to harm him, much less incapacitate him. But he'll understand exactly what you were trying to do. And he's very likely to punish you for your audacity. So keep your knees where they belong. There's only one way to kick an assaulter's testicles with any chance of success. That's by using a *sho-do-kan* karate front snap kick, in which your instep smashes into his testicles. But even this kick works only if the assaulter cooperates by spreading his legs. Now, can you see yourself walking down a street at dusk, being assaulted, and saying to your assaulter, "Would you please spread?"

But what about my fists, you say? I know your boyfriend or husband has told you that if you're ever assaulted, smash your attacker in the groin with your fist. Well, he doesn't realize that the testicle area of a man's groin—the testes themselves—are tiny, compared with the large surrounding thigh area.

When your boyfriend gives that sort of advice, he's probably thinking, How can she miss? Well, if men were built the way they'd like to think they are, they'd have to walk around with a wheelbarrow in front of them.

And remember our test: Will he know what you've tried?

If you've ever even glanced through a book on self-defense, you've probably come across the statement that you can incapacitate a man with a *fist or elbow blow to the solar plexus*. The truth is, you can kill him—if you can find the solar plexus and hit it hard enough.

Solar plexus is Latin for "center of nerves." This major nerve "substation" is located just below the xiphoid process, at the bottom of the sternum, which is the bony structure that runs down the middle of the chest from the neck to the upper abdomen.

The trouble with the solar plexus as a target—outside of the fact that it's probably moving (since he is)—is that the exposed area is about half the diameter of a dime. And I've yet to see one that's marked with a bull's-eye. What would you say the odds are that you can hit it—one in a thousand? Let's be generous. Let's say one in ten. What happens in the other nine cases? How many chances do you think your attacker is going to give you?

My point is, if you aim for your assaulter's solar plexus, you'll probably miss—especially with the elbow (a technique that's usually highly recommended for situations in which you're grabbed from behind). You'd probably have trouble finding it with a probing pin. So you're hitting him on the chest. Because of his large pectoral muscles, you probably won't hurt him. If he's skinny, you may smash his chest. But how are you to know he's skinny—reach back and feel? And what do you think he'll be doing while you're hitting him? He'll be tearing you apart. At best, you'll crack one or two of his ribs. That's hardly incapacitating. Men can—and have—played a full game of football with injuries much worse than that. A man with cracked ribs can rape you just about as easily as a man whose ribs are perfect, and he's likely to throw in a beating for good measure, since you've been violent.

The Adam's apple is another spot on the man's body that's often thought of as vulnerable. You probably have been told to strike your attacker there with your fist or the side of the hand. The truth is, very few men can be instantly incapacitated by a blow to the Adam's apple. They may feel pain, they may gag, but they'll be fully able to take instant revenge. In addition, we are once again talking about an extremely tiny area—given the total area of the neck. Men with a well-developed neck will probably feel little pain at all. Besides, the assaulter is emotionally disturbed, not stupid. As with the other methods we've talked about, he'll understand what you've just tried to do, and react with more violence.

If you've really done some reading in self-defense, you

may have come across the statement that you can put a man out by hitting him with the heel of the palm of your hand at the *base of his nose*. True enough. The difficulty, once again, is that you're aiming at an area the size of the head of a hatpin—where the upper lip and the base of the nose meet. To be effective, you must strike this area at an upward angle of 47 to 48 degrees, with at least forty pounds of pressure. If you can hit the area properly, your blow will be effective, since you'll be driving the assaulter's nasal bones into his brain. But as you're grappling and trying to get him to tilt his head back and hold still, and as you're ramming the heel of your palm into his chin and cheeks and forehead, trying to find the elusive area, what do you think he's going to be doing? Your chances of incapacitating your assaulter with a blow to the base of his nose are just about zero. But even if they were fifty-fifty, *chances* are just what you don't want to take in the assault situation.

Many assaulters initiate their attack with a choke hold, either standing in front of their victim with both hands around her neck or standing behind her with the forearm of one arm around her neck.

When I ask my lecture audiences what to do in either of these situations, I usually get the following responses.

For the choke hold in front: "My boyfriend says to shove my arms up against the inside of his forearms and knock them away." This is ludicrous. First, it assumes you'll be as strong as your assaulter. Usually, this is not true. Second, even if it does work, you've committed yourself—and what do you do now? You've just verified his reason for choking you in the first place. He did it because he thought you might be violent and because he wanted to protect himself. Now, he's got to double his effort. Where does that leave you?

As for the choke hold from behind, you may have heard

that you will break a man's eardrums by slapping both hands across his ears. That's possible. But once again; you're verifying his belief that you might be violent, which is why he is choking you in the first place. On the other hand, ask yourself how many times out of a hundred you could accurately cup both of your hands over both of his ears. The ear opening is just too small for your chances to rate even one in a hundred.

Women are often told that if they're grabbed by an assaulter, they should *stomp down on his instep*, his metatarsal bones. A good, hard stomp in the right spot *can* break the metatarsal bones, but a man can still rape with one set of metatarsals. The injury won't incapacitate him, and worse, it's an area almost impossible to target and hit.

Every one of these kicks and blows fails the test. You can't be certain they'll incapacitate the attacker every time. Even worse, each of them irrevocably commits your behavior, ensuring that the assault will include violence.

But can the same be said if you've taken the trouble to learn karate, judo, jujitsu, aikido or savate (French foot boxing)? After all, these martial arts are considered by many to be the ultimate defense against any type of assault.

Let's define them and see. Perhaps the most famous of the martial arts is judo. And it isn't a martial art at all, it's a sport. In 1895 the Japanese took all of the deadly elements out of a martial art known as jujitsu and invented a sport called judo. In judo, two people pair off in an eight-yard by eight-yard ring, grasp each other by the lapels of a bathrobelike uniform called a *gi* and practice throwing techniques. To master this sport, a person must study for at least a year and a half. In the first six weeks to three months, he will learn only one thing—how to fall.

Proficiency in judo requires considerable strength, especially in fingers, forearms, shoulders and legs. You'll have no guarantee that you can handle a husky 200-pounder—size is also an important element in judo. Even in tournaments, judoists are paired off according to weight and even height. Lightweights aren't pitted against heavyweights, since strength and size play so much of a role in the sport.

This is why judo has limited value in self-defense. To be certain of victory, you must always be sure that your opponent is not only less skilled than you, but that he also doesn't outweigh you outrageously and isn't a great deal stronger. And the assault confrontation doesn't usually offer such a choice.

That's not to say judo is valueless, even in self-defense. It can help anyone attain control, timing, suppleness and balance. Judo skills are especially valuable when combined with a knowledge of other martial arts. And the best judoists are quite skilled at self-defense. But judo is the long route to self-defense, one that probably shouldn't be attempted by anyone who hasn't a *lot* of time to spend at it.

Size and strength aren't so vital when it comes to the "real" martial arts: karate, from Japan, and its stylistic and geographical variations: kung (or gung) fu, from China; ishin-ru, from Okinawa; and tae kwan do, from Korea; and aikido and jujitsu itself.

Karate is as much a philosophy as a martial art. Its first aim is to avoid confrontation altogether. To this end, karate-ists blend all of their mental and physical capabilities into an effective fighting unit. They use balance, speed, maneuverability, profound awareness and perception to evade attack. This failing, they block what blows come their way, relying on an extraordinary suppleness which they achieve through total mental and physical self-control. If the danger persists, they strike out, but mostly with their feet (since legs, after all, are a foot and a half longer and eleven times stronger than arms), focusing their power on single, specific "pressure points," or nerve "centers," on their attackers' bodies.

The advantage of karate is that it can give a person the ability to handle himself in nearly any situation, even against gangs, even against opponents with weapons, except projectile weapons. The main disadvantage: it takes years to become really proficient in all aspects of karate, though simplified forms can be learned more quickly.

Jujitsu, a creation of the Japanese, consists of hundreds of different defenses, each designed to counter a specific attack from an opponent. It emphasizes throws and maneuvers that force an opponent to use his body weight and strength against himself. It also uses punches and kicks. Each defense must be memorized, according to the attack it is meant to counter.

The advantage of jujitsu is that it can be (and often is, especially in the armed forces or police) taught piecemeal. A person can fairly quickly learn a few basic defenses. The disadvantage is the many moves you must learn if you are to master the art. That can take years. Meanwhile, the novice, assaulted by a guy with a weird limp, may hesitate between defense no. 22 and defense no. 63. By the time he or she decides, the fight may be over.

For all of their differences, the martial arts have a lot in common. A layman watching a martial arts demonstration would have trouble distinguishing between judo, jujitsu and aikido (a physical self-defense system that stresses body movement, timing, control and balance). Karate would be easier to identify, since it involves more straight striking with arms and, especially, legs.

I can state my opinion of the martial arts simply enough. As far as I'm concerned, mankind has never devised a more effective means of self-defense than the martial arts. But they aren't the best way to prevent rape. They require too many sacrifices to learn them. Most people are too busy to take six weeks or six months—whatever you and your instructor feel is adequate—to learn enough for effective self-defense.

I encourage everyone, man and woman alike, to take a good martial art self-defense course. (Personally, I think karate has an edge. It can be learned more quickly than the others and is somewhat more practical.) But I have found that it is the rare individual who is willing to endure the tremendous amount of hard work, patience, determination, practice and mental anguish which goes into learning these magnificent moves and techniques.

Furthermore, even when used by someone who is skilled and knowledgeable, they fail all of our common-sense laws of assault safety: Do nothing that can hurt you; Don't antagonize; Don't commit your behavior. If you attempt to use the martial arts on your assaulter, and he turns out to be better at them than you, they can hurt you. Certainly, their use does antagonize. And there's no question that it commits your behavior. Once you've launched into using the martial arts, there's no way you can reverse yourself. You've added violence to the assault and there's a good chance your assaulter will return your move in kind.

In at least one case I know of, a rapist was evidently infuriated by the very fact that women were learning karate. Maybe he felt he was somehow being challenged or put down. He'd wait outside the local YWCA, which was offering the course, until the students left. Then he'd waylay one of them, rape her and beat her up—karate style, of course.

The lesson here: no matter how perfect your knowledge of self-defense, you cannot be sure it will save you from rape. The rapist may have equal or greater knowledge. He may have partners. He may have weapons. Certainly, he will have the advantage of surprise.

In September 1973 a young woman who was skilled in karate was raped and murdered in New Jersey. A bloody men's T-shirt was found near the scene of the crime and police theorized that the woman was able to injure the man somewhat. Some consolation! He beat her up badly and strangled her to death. So study karate if you like—but should you find yourself in the assault situation, use the principles in this book *first*. If for some reason, they don't help you, they can't harm you. You can always use your karate knowledge then. Besides, if you follow my advice, you will be using *mental* karate.

Weapons. I hear constantly that if women only carried weapons, they'd be safe from attack. And I've heard a wide variety of weapons recommended, from objects a woman might normally carry—a fingernail file, or a rattail comb, a hat pin, keys, or even a book—to such out-and-out weapons as tear gas pens, knives or revolvers.

Where would you normally carry such weapons? Assuming you don't wear holsters, you'd keep them in your purse. Unfortunately, the first thing most women do when they're assaulted is drop their purses—if only from the shock of the assault. So there she is, on all fours, at ten o'clock on a dark night, a hundred and eighty pounds of man crawling all over her, searching for her purse.

Let's say that you're an exception, that you hold onto your purse and you have time to withdraw one of the more highly touted weapons of recent years, a tear gas pen (instead of a wad of tissues or some gum wrappers). There's only one problem with a tear gas pen: you have to be sure your assaulter approaches you from downwind. Otherwise, you, not he, will be the one getting the gas—unless you can persuade him to rape you from the other direction. Also, too many times, the woman who attempts to use tear gas or Mace ends up both raped and gassed. Actually, the amount of tear gas in one of those pens is so small that, in the first place, it isn't likely to do much more than annoy the assaulter. Secondly, it will dissipate in the atmosphere too quickly to have any lasting effect. Then, too, there's no way to prevent the assaulter from moving away from the tear gas—his feet aren't nailed to the ground.

Another weapon I've often heard recommended is your ordinary, everyday hardcover book. Just carry one of these, some self-defense experts say, and you're safe from attack. If confronted by an assaulter, bash him on the head. If that's enough to knock out your assaulter, fine. But if it isn't, you've committed your behavior, you've made sure your encounter is violent, and you've done something that can end up harming you.

I could say the same thing about a host of other weapons you might normally carry with you—a comb, a file, a ballpoint pen, a set of keys or even an umbrella with a sharpened point. All of them will work in rare instances. But if they don't, God help you. Last year, at one of my lectures, I asked the audience, "What would you do if you were assaulted?" One woman spoke out immediately. "I'd grab anything I could out of my purse and stab him with it!" There were murmurs of approval. Then I looked over at one of the men in the audience and asked, "And what would you do if she did that to you?" He said, "I'd kill her." There was dead silence.

I asked this woman, "How many times out of a hundred could you stab a man in an area that would completely incapacitate him?" And I even gave her the benefit of the doubt. I allowed that she would be able to find a formidable weapon in her purse—a pen, and not a pack of tissues. "Let us assume you are able to get something sharp and pointed. How many times out of a hundred could you stab him in an area that would completely incapacitate him? Twenty-five times or even ten times out of a hundred?" The woman said she guessed less than five—which isn't very good odds for the other ninety-five trying it. Even if it works forty times out of a hundred—impossible—my question is, "What do you do the other sixty times?"

The woman is stabbing him with a pen and she stabs him in the cheek. This obviously doesn't incapacitate him. What does she say to him now?

It is very easy to tell her what to do in the assault. What's hard is to tell her what to do if whatever she has already done fails. And that's what this program is all about.

A weapon has one instant effect in the assault situation; it immediately and irrevocably initiates violence. It forces an immediate decision on the assaulter. He must either run—or attack. And the woman won't know which he's going to do until he does it. Is that a chance she wants to take, considering that her life may be at stake? In any case, most of the time, women don't manage to get out of their purses what weapons they might have. And assaulters often see such fumbling for what it is—a search for weapons. More important, nine times out of ten, he'll simply take the weapon away from the woman and use it on her.

Not only can depending on a weapon hurt the woman physically, it can hurt her emotionally, in a way that's not immediately obvious. Carrying a weapon tends to breed false confidence. The woman (or man, for that matter) who carries one comes to depend on it, to believe it will protect in dangerous situations. What happens, then, if she's assaulted when she doesn't have the weapon or if she can't get to it? The result is, instead of one, *two* emotionally unstable people: the rapist and his victim. And no woman can handle a rapist if she's lost her emotional stability. It seems to me weapons are always wrong, except in that one instance: immediate defense of your life. First, to be effective you have to have your weapon with you at all times, ready to use. And anything that isn't permanently attached to your body won't be with you at *all* times.

Second, you have to know exactly how to handle the weapon—and be *willing* to use it. That means that you've practiced and it also means that you'll be able to call on a violent streak of your own if you're attacked.

Third, your attacker would have to permit you to use your weapon on him. Remember, in an assault, you're the one who's being surprised. The assaulter is ready to make his move, ready for nearly anything you might do, including your attempt to use some object as a weapon.

Fourth, you would have to be sure that your weapon could incapacitate your attacker every time. Even if you were carrying a knife or a revolver, you might miss.

Fifth, you'd have to be certain he wasn't carrying a weapon himself. If he were, and you tried to use a weapon on him, his first act would be to finish you off before you did it to him.

Sixth, you'd have to have some alternate plan in mind if your weapon didn't work. This strikes me as impossible. By using a weapon, you've committed your behavior. You can't yell, "Cut. Retake." You're not the director of this little drama, you're only one of the players.

Even when a woman has to go into a bad area, where there are a lot of rapes, she should not carry a loaded pistol or any other weapon because she can't be sure of protecting herself. If the attacker comes from the rear, the chance to use the weapon may be over before the woman even knew she had one. Even when a man approaches from the front, how can she be sure he's going to attack her? He may want a dime for a cup of coffee, or directions to the bus stop. If she shoots the man who approaches her, she'd better be sure he's an attacker or she could spend time in jail for manslaughter. Let's assume, generously as usual, that her attacker has approached from the front and he's announced, "Lady, you're about to be raped." Now she has to be sure that when she fires her gun, she hits him—not herself, not some innocent bystander, not a fireplug or an apartment building. That will be the hardest thing of all, unless she's really proficient with that pistol.

There are booklets and leaflets and newspaper and magazine articles everywhere about weapons written by people who really want to help but don't know the answers. Out of frustration they advocate some really ridiculous ideas. One such booklet advises women to place their car keys between their fingers and scratch at their assailants' faces. How many times out of a hundred do you think a woman could incapacitate someone this way? Remember, she can't *just* hurt him. This kind of advice actually results in killing women.

To add to the bad news, *running* isn't a good defense against assault either, unless the woman is absolutely sure she can get to safety. The rapist's reaction will be about the same as if she struggles. He'll knock her down and keep hitting until he's sure she won't run again. Perhaps sometimes she'll get away, particularly if she's only a few feet away from genuine safety. A dorm, a doorman, a crowd of people, a good solid door with a strong lock will protect her, if the assaulter is a fair distance from her when she realizes an assault is about to begin—150 yards, say. In that case, I *do* advocate running.

Nevertheless, it seems to me foolhardy to run. Most men can outrun most women. That's why there are separate events at the Olympics for male and female runners. An assaulter isn't interested in raping fast-moving targets, so he'll probably do what's necessary to make sure you stop running.

I'm sorry to have to tell you that *crying*, pleading and small talk won't guarantee that a rapist will release his victim. There's a good chance it will win her a beating. Remember, the rapist is emotionally unstable, not stupid.

In one case I know of, a young woman was standing on a street corner waiting for her boyfriend. A man leaped out of the bushes, grabbed her and dragged her behind some shrubs. The woman pleaded with her assaulter, "Please don't do anything to me," she said. "I'm a virgin. I'm only eighteen." Then she started crying.

She didn't realize it, but she was antagonizing her assaulter. By saying she was a virgin, she was putting herself above him, in effect saying, "I'm pure, don't defile me." Further, she was telling him he had the chance of a lifetime, the rapists' dream, the opportunity to belittle, humiliate and degrade someone fresh and innocent, who epitomized the women he felt had been putting him down. (But sometimes a woman whom rapists see as vulgar or loose enrages them even more.)

The young woman kept begging and crying. "I've already stayed out too long," she told the assaulter. "My mother will be worried. She always worries about me, ever since Dad died. She hates to be alone in the house. Please let me go."

If the rapist hadn't been interested until then, those last remarks got attention. "You're lying," he said shrewdly.

"No, no," the woman protested. "It's true. We live at . . ." She gave him the address.

"Well, let's just see about that," said her assaulter.

In the end, he raped both the young woman and her mother, and beat up both of them.

"She treated me as if I had no sense," he told the police who captured him. "The little bitch played games with me, then she teased me."

Fainting is another action that is wrong for several reasons. While it isn't antagonistic, it does commit the woman's behavior. She can't very well unfaint, at least not at

will. Besides, like all the other techniques I've discussed so
far, though fainting may work sometimes, it won't work all
the time. If the woman faints, the rapist may walk away,
having no interest in an inert female. Or he may run, afraid
he's hurt you. But on the other hand, he may rape you
repeatedly, then angered at your lack of response, beat you
up. Or worse. And I'm not going to recommend something
in my book that might cause you to never wake up.

"But fainting is involuntary," you say. "How can I stop
myself, if that's the way I'm going to react?" Fainting occurs when someone meets a situation she (or he) is entirely unprepared for, and is bereft of ways to handle it or
the confidence that she can improvise a way.

The next four chapters of this book are devoted to
methods by which you can avoid rape or prevent bodily
harm if you are assaulted. These chapters prepare you for
what might happen to you and tell you how to handle it. If
you read them, you'll have no reason to faint if assaulted
and the part of your mind that triggers that response will
know that.

Total surrender is also the wrong thing if you're assaulted. Though no rapist will see that reaction as antagonistic, and though you can always change your mind, you
are abdicating all responsibility during the attack, including the responsibility you have to yourself. To mentally
and physically surrender completely is to resign from the
human race. It's like hanging over a cliff, clinging to a
branch or rock and just letting go, instead of trying to at
least figure a way to climb back up. Partially surrendering,
as a stall to give yourself time to find a way to safely react,
is as far as surrendering should go. And only you know
when that point is.

4

Escape and Evasion

Some women, when assaulted, are raped, beaten, mutilated, even murdered. Others escape not only without injury, but also, fairly frequently, without even being sexually attacked. Why?

That was the question I set out to answer ten years ago. The key to rape prevention, I felt, was to be found with the women who had successfully handled an assault, avoiding rape or other harm.

In fact, it wasn't as simple as that. In many cases, women were hard put to say just what the assaulter had intended—rape, purse-snatching, a hostile shove in a crowded area or something totally innocent. And some were equally hard put to say what had discouraged the attack.

To confuse matters, there was a large group of women who had done all of the things I say are wrong—and got out of attacks anyhow. But that's not surprising, I suppose. Screaming, struggling, crying *do work*—about half the time. These cases didn't offer me much, since I was interested in finding methods that worked *all* the time, or if they didn't work, at least didn't harm the victim.

I was left with a group of incidents in which an assaulter had accosted a woman, announced or demonstrated his intention to rape her and beat her up, and then did neither. These were genuine assaults, of that I was sure, but the victims had escaped rape or bodily injury.

It would simplify matters a lot if after studying these cases, I could say that the women who defeated their attackers all used one of a dozen different tricks. Then a woman could memorize the list, and that would be that.

In fact, the women who repelled their attackers used an astonishing variety of tactics, so diverse that it's hard to categorize them.

For all the different tactics, though, the successful "non-victims" *did act* in a particular way during the assault. They exhibited several distinct, discernible behavior patterns. And, taken together, these patterns make up the core of my approach to preventing rape or injury: the five principles of rape prevention.

These principles are a distillation of the behavior that has saved thousands of women from rape and injury. They aren't recommendations which specify exactly what to do in each circumstance. Rather, these principles describe the understanding and attitude every potential assault victim must achieve if she is to save herself from rape and bodily harm. She may feel that some or all of them are beyond her ability now, but she won't feel that way by the time she has studied this program:

1. Retain—or regain—your emotional stability.

In other words, keep your cool. Every assault consists of three elements: the assaulter, the environment and you.

If you're emotionally unstable, you're not going to be able to read the rapist, or take effective or rational action against him. You're going to miss those clues that if spotted, would help you slip out of danger. Further, you're not going to be aware of your environment and its dangers or opportunities.

The women who have successfully dealt with their rapists have capitalized on their stability and their rapists' lack of it. That doesn't mean they were as calm as Indian yogis. Every one of them was upset to one degree or another. Some panicked initially, only to regain their control after a while. But the plain fact is that when a woman maintains emotional stability in the assault situation, she has control. All she has to do is use it.

2. *Treat the rapist as a human being.*

Even when emotionally disturbed, people tend to live up to what other people expect of them. Treat a person as a mad dog and he'll do his best not to disappoint you. Call him a disgusting brute and, very likely, he'll *be* disgusting and *act* brutally. Act as if he's inhuman and he won't feel the need to stay within normal human constraints.

I'm not saying it's easy to treat an assaulter as a human being. A woman will tend to see her attacker as a leering monster, no matter what he looks like or how he acts. On the other side, it won't be easy for an assaulter to understand that he's being treated as a human being, since, most probably, he's rarely been accorded the respect every human being deserves.

Nevertheless, if you're going to avoid rape or injury, you'll have to treat your attacker as a human being and you'll have to make sure he gets the message. The women who have survived assaults and avoided rape have done this consistently. In one case I know of, a woman stopped an assault by doing nothing more than this. The results were surprising.

The assaulter, as it happened, was an exceptionally

bright fellow, a man who, until a few months earlier, had earned a perfect 4.0 average through seven semesters of college. But during his last semester he flunked all his courses and began to assault. Obviously, something traumatic had happened between the seventh and eighth semesters. On checking, I found that when he went home for the semester break, he discovered that his entire family—his mother, father, two sisters and a brother—had been killed in an auto accident that morning.

Instead of feeling grieved or depressed, his reaction was to feel persecuted. He felt the whole world was against him. Since we tend to support the attitudes we form, he went back to school and twisted every relationship to prove he was right. But further evidence of this persecution was necessary, so without being aware of what he was doing, he purposely flunked his courses, and got his proof.

The evening he received his grades he went out walking and came upon a cat, which he kicked. The cat hissed at him and he kicked it to death (he later said he felt the cat was against him). Still later, he came upon a small dog. Again, he lashed out. The dog squealed in terror, but the young man interpreted this, too, as rejection. He started kicking the dog, stopping only when it had lost consciousness. (Note that he stopped beating the dog when it stopped moving.)

Several hours later, a young woman almost ran into him. He grabbed her by the arm, expecting she would scream or repulse him—as had the cat, the dog, his friends and his professors these last months, or so he had perceived. He was all ready to slam her to the ground and beat her into submission. Instead, something interesting happened.

Later the woman told me the story. "I'm not sure what I said at that moment," she related. "I don't even know that I said anything at all. But I remember what I thought:

Here is a person in trouble. Somehow, I must have conveyed my feelings."

What started as an assault now turned into a conversation. The man ended up telling the woman that she was "the first live thing that wasn't against me in the last nine months."

Strangely—or maybe not so strangely, depending on your point of view—they started dating. It turned out that they had a lot in common. With a small amount of informal counseling and a lot of emotional support from the woman, the man faced his tragedy, saw it for what it was, and adjusted. Today, he's probably as healthy as you or I—maybe healthier, since he did have some professional help, which just about every one of us could use from time to time. And the two of them are now married.

3. *Gain his confidence.*

Few women realize it, but in general, the rapist is just as frightened during the assault as his victim. You see, until the assaulter has done his deed and gone, and possibly even afterward, you represent a considerable threat to his security.

He worries that you may scream and draw attention. He's afraid you might struggle or you might have a weapon, in which case *he* could be the one who ends up hurt. He fears that you will report the assault to the police, perhaps identify him and send him to prison. He's worried that you're not going to give him what he wants, what he thinks he needs. He's terrified that you'll be repelled by him, or put him down. He may even be frightened by his own impulses.

For your own safety, you have to ease his fears. You have to find some way to reassure him so that he knows you represent neither a mental nor a physical threat to him.

Unless you gain his confidence, you will be in danger throughout the assault. Like all of us, the rapist deals with threats in just two ways: fight or flight. If he sees you as a threat, he may run. But he may just as readily strike out, even kill you.

If your assaulter is carrying a weapon, you'll have to gain his confidence if you're ever to find a way out of the assault situation. Only when he is convinced that you cannot or will not do him any harm in any way will he let down his guard and put down his weapon.

For the women who have defeated their assaulters, gaining the man's confidence has been an essential step in gaining their own freedom, unmarked and unharmed.

4. *Go along until you can safely react.*

Your impulse, when assaulted, may be to act in immediate self-defense. That impulse could cost you everything if you follow it. The rapist is sure to see such behavior as antagonistic, something to counter in whatever way he can.

Remember, at least in the beginning everything is going the assaulter's way. He has chosen the time, the place and the method of assault. He has chosen you. And as for you, you've had little or no warning whatever. You're certain to be badly surprised, perhaps shocked.

That's why you must give the impression of going along with your assaulter, for a while, anyhow. This will give you further time to regain your emotional stability, if you've been shaken, as you will be. For anywhere from a few seconds to a few hours, depending on the circumstances, you're going to have to stall, by doing what he says or by giving every indication you're about to. I'm not saying that you should go along sexually, though that may be necessary to a degree if your assaulter is armed, ready to harm you physically, or you're in a group rape situation. What you're really doing here is using sex as a weapon, as a means to stall. Your need to go along will end, when you see or devise a chance to safely react.

Now, just when, during an assault, is it safe for you to react? It's safe when your assaulter's guard is down. It's safe when the rapist is mentally occupied with his anticipation of things to come. (And that, after all, is one of the reasons he's assaulted you.) It's safe when the environment has changed in some way, either through your efforts or by happenstance. It's safe when you figure out just which approach will work on this particular assaulter.

Since no two assaults are exactly alike, no one can tell you in advance precisely which moment will be safe. But by the very nature of the assault, I can assure you such a moment *will* come, at least once. Probably there will be several. Thousands of women have found this moment and acted upon it, with exactly the desired results.

5. Use your imagination and your good judgment.

It's one thing to find the right moment and quite another to know what to do when you find it. Most of the women who have come out safely after an assault didn't reach back into their memories when they spotted that right moment, hoping to recall and use some standardized technique. Instead, they depended on their imagination, taking everything into account—their knowledge of assaults, their own limitations and capabilities, the character of the assaulter so far as they knew it, and the environment. They invented tactics that met the situation. They improvised.

In one case that was reported to me, two women who had heard my lecture three days earlier were walking in a New York City park. Two men began to follow them. The women at first walked faster. So did the men. Then the women slowed down. The men did too. The women told me that they really weren't sure what to do. They said they remembered from my lecture that they should do nothing that could be perceived as antagonistic or violent. But they weren't sure what they *should* do.

Well, they kept their heads, nonetheless, and tried to use what information they had. For instance, they noticed that the men seemed more interested in following them than actually confronting them. The way these women saw it, the men seemed interested in "just" picking them up, for a starter, anyhow.

So the women decided that the best way to handle the situation was to turn them off sexually. They began to pet and pat each other's bottoms and kiss each other.

How did the men react? They turned around and took off. From what they said as they left, it was obvious that they were disgusted by what they'd seen. They were repelled, in both senses of the word.

No one had ever advised either of these women to act like a lesbian in the face of an assault (and incidentally, they weren't lesbians). No one could have foreseen that they would have faced assault while together.

These women used their imagination. And they followed all of the other principles of rape prevention. They didn't panic. They treated their would-be assaulters as people— or, to be more precise, as men who wouldn't be interested in homosexual women. They did nothing antagonistic and they put on as convincing an act as they could. And they seized the safest moment of all to react—before the assault began.

They did one more thing: they used good judgment. They didn't attempt to do something that was beyond their capabilities or something that was unbelievable. For some women this kind of performance would be impossible. Those women shouldn't try it because it wouldn't work for them. It would be seen as nothing more than a ruse, and an insulting one at that. In the same way, quiet women shouldn't suddenly burst out into conversation and shy women shouldn't try to appear bold and extroverted. Imagination, then, is vital, but it must be tempered with judgment. No woman should ever attempt something that is so totally out of character that she really has no chance to pull it off. Perhaps, from the examples that will follow, you will find a tactic that could be the right thing for you to do if you're assaulted. If so, don't hesitate to use it. If not, don't hesitate to use your imagination and good judgment and come up with something new. There are countless techniques that no one has thought of yet that *will work*.

Though the five principles of rape prevention can be stated separately, they're so closely linked as to be inseparable. How can you treat the rapist as a human being if you've lost your own emotional stability? How can you gain his confidence if you don't treat him as a human being? How can you wait until you can safely react if you haven't gained his confidence? And last, are you using your imagination and good judgment if you react when it's not safe?

Are you ready to go out and do battle with an assaulter now? Of course not. Going over a list of rules—or even memorizing it—isn't the same as putting the rules into practice. That's especially true when we're talking about an assault, the sort of situation that tends to throw even the calmest mind off the track.

Let's carefully examine an assault, from the victim's point of view, from beginning to end to see how to apply these principles so that the victim, not the assailant, wins.

Suppose you're walking alone along a quiet side street near the business district of your town. It's nearly ten o'clock and the stores are closed. There isn't a soul in sight and even passing cars are a rarity. But you're not worried. You're not even thinking about the possibility of assault. You're considering the dress you saw earlier, wondering if you should go back and buy it tomorrow. You're thinking about a book you want to read. You're hoping you win your tennis match this weekend. Your oldest son's birthday is coming up and you're wondering what you should get him.

At first you think nothing of the steps behind you. There's nothing extraordinary about them, except that they're getting steadily louder. A shadow of doubt crosses your mind, but it's a small one, easily dismissed. People have a right to be walking here. There's no reason you should have the street to yourself. In fact, it's good to have company.

Suddenly you find yourself walking a little faster. And wishing you had even more company. The footsteps are getting closer now, and louder. For a moment you allow yourself to think the thought: Is someone after me? No, the answer comes back instantly, that only happens in the newspapers. This is too nice a neighborhood for that.

You grit your teeth and step up the pace, your heart beating rapidly now. Perhaps fifty feet ahead of you, the stores peter out and there's a small park. Beyond that, a block or two away, there are more stores and a row of bright street lights. You aim for them.

You never get there. Somewhere alongside the park, the footsteps merge with yours. Mustering all your courage, you turn to confront whoever it is who's following you and find yourself roughly grabbed by both arms, then half picked up and half dragged into the bushes, out of sight of the street.

Things take on an other-worldly quality now, as if life has suddenly turned into a slow-motion movie. You are simultaneously convinced that this is nothing more than a nightmare and certain that you're undergoing the beginnings of a horrible, dangerous experience.

Whether you're aware of it or not, you're now having your first reaction to the assault. Without so much as thinking about it, you've probably done one of three things: screamed, lashed out at your assailant or entered into a mild state of shock. A woman who hasn't read this book might also faint, if her unconscious mind says she has no resources whatever with which to deal with the attack. How you initially react to the assault depends on your life experiences, your heredity, your temperament, your mood, possibly even the environment you're in. Whether or not you survive the assault depends not so much on that initial reaction but on what you do *next*, right after that initial reaction provided it doesn't last too long.

Two of those conditioned responses to the assault are not useful to you and should be stopped and reversed as soon as you become aware of them. I'm talking about screaming or lashing out at the assaulter. The moment you know you're doing one or the other of these two things, stop instantly and start apologizing. "I'm sorry, I was startled," you might say. Or, "I didn't mean to hit you." Or, "I thought it was someone else." (The implication here: he's all right, but you wouldn't have wanted anyone else to do that.)

But why on earth should you apologize to a rapist? This is why: you're in a difficult, maybe even desperate situation; what you need to do is to halt any violence before it begins, to keep the danger at a minimum. If you can trade an apology or two for wholeness of limb or body, you're making a good deal.

As for how to do it, say what I've suggested or anything else that comes into your mind. Act the same way you would if you came around the corner and crashed into someone carrying an armload of bundles, knocking him down, sending the bundles flying.

Will he accept your apology? Well, he's probably not going to say, "Oh, that's all right, I understand." But it will show him that he doesn't have to hit you to get you to shut up, or knock you unconscious to stop you from struggling. Remember, many an argument has cooled down when the *wronged* person apologizes.

Incidentally, this is the time to face your assaulter, and not with your eyes closed. (The only exception to this is if you perceive that he doesn't want you to see his face.) If you don't look at him, you'll probably imagine him to be much worse than he is. After all, how bad can a human being really look? Furthermore, you will be better able to "read" him—and that's *all*-important.

"But what happens if I'm simply paralyzed with fear?" you may ask. This is the *safest* initial response of all—a simple lack of response. That's what I mean when I say you might go into mild shock.

If this is what happens to you—and it probably will—accept it. Welcome it, in fact. You're apparently one of those people who have been conditioned to respond to an assault in the safest possible manner. If you can extend the state for a while, so much the better. This period of being dazed or paralyzed or surprised is a gift to you from your brain. It saves you from making such mistakes as screaming or struggling, and besides giving your assaulter no excuse to start beating you, it gives you time to think and adjust to your situation. You need time to catch your breath, to become aware of what's happening to you, to set up your defenses, to figure a way out of the situation, to shift the surprise from you to him. You should continue to act dazed even after your initial shock has passed. You're buying time for yourself that way. It will seem like long minutes, but it will probably be only a few seconds before you have control over your actions again.

As you become aware of your situation, one of the first feelings you'll be conscious of is fear. Expect that. It's natural, it's healthy, it's even useful. Women often ask if they should hide their fear from their assaulter. I guess they're remembering what they heard in some old African lion hunt movie in which the great white hunter tells the beautiful woman—as the lion approaches, salivating—that she'll be fine if she doesn't show her fear.

First of all, I don't think you'll be able to hide your fear if you try. Second, your assaulter is *not* an animal, he's a human being. He understands fear. He can empathize with it. Furthermore, if you show him you're afraid, you're telling him he is powerful and strong. And if you tell him clearly enough, he won't have to prove it to you. The man who feels powerful and strong is much less likely to consider you a threat than the man who is almost overwhelmed by his own fear and feelings of weakness. If he thinks you're no threat to him, he's that much less likely to beat you up, or to use whatever weapon he might be carrying.

Sometimes the simple expression of fear can stop an assault at the beginning. Last year, during a West Coast radio show on rape, a rapist called in and told of what it was like from his side. He described what happened during a particular assault:

"I grabbed her from behind and turned her around and pushed her against the wall. She didn't have much chance to get away from me. She tried. I pulled her back and hit her several times in the face quite hard and she stopped resisting and she said, 'All right, just don't hurt me.' All of a sudden, a thought came into my head: my God, this woman is a human being. I came to my senses and saw that I was hurting this woman, that a person was involved, that it was not an actress in a movie . . ."

He let her go, unharmed, unraped, *because* she showed him she was afraid.

Don't be afraid to reveal your fear. Don't be afraid of *being* afraid. It shows respect for something or someone. Only when fear becomes obsession is it no longer useful or healthy—it becomes an emotional disturbance. But healthy fear of assaults can be put to good use. Once you pass through the initial moments of shock, your fear can even help you, by producing adrenaline and spurring you on to find the way out of the problem you're facing.

So there you are, in the bushes, still on your feet, but wobbly, the attacker's strong hands clutching you. (The truth is that many rapists are pathetic physical specimens. That's another good reason to take a look at him. He may not be so formidable.) You're just at the point where the shock is wearing off a bit. You're beginning to realize that this is an assault, that he's a rapist and that you, unless you do something about it, are the rapee.

What you need here, more than anything else, is time to think. You need to stall. There are several things you can do to get yourself time, without being beaten up in the bargain.

First, as we've discussed, you can simply continue doing what you're doing now—acting dazed or shocked. You can appear to be speechless with surprise. The rapist will see that you can't start obeying orders, at least not yet. You'll have at least a few moments and perhaps longer to get the wheels turning upstairs.

Second, you can go limp. If you go limp, your attacker suddenly finds he's holding a hundred pounds or more of inert female. He's got to do something with that dead weight. Like putting it down, for example. By going limp, you haven't committed your behavior, you haven't done anything irreversible. What you have done is to become inanimate, lifeless, thereby reducing your value to the rapist, who is looking for contact with a living, breathing, moving human being. Rarely he wants you inanimate. What you've also done is to give yourself time to think.

"But what if my attacker perceives that as hostile and antagonistic and noncooperative?" you might ask. "What if he says, 'Baby, you start responding—or else'?" Well then, you may have to start responding. You still can, you know.

He may be less likely to make that kind of demand if you've gone one step further: if you've faked a faint. The advantage of pretending to faint is that the rapist might feel he's hurt you seriously, and that may not be what he had in mind. In fact, he will usually turn and run. (If you really faint, it's irreversible. You've lost the ability to think, to adapt your defense to what he does.)

After mentioning this idea at one of my lectures, a woman came up to me and told me that she'd heard my lecture when I was there last year and used this very thought. She'd been grabbed one day while walking along the street. She was thrown into an alley between two buildings. In being thrown, she hit her forehead on one of the buildings and scratched it, drawing a little blood. Then she fell down. Instead of screaming or struggling, she just lay there, eyes closed. She wasn't really hurt, but a single drop of blood trickled down her cheek from the scratch. Her assaulter stood over her for a moment, said, "Oh my God, I've killed her," then darted out of the alley and ran away.

Another time, a woman told me that she was pushed back over some bushes. She fell down, but hardly hard enough to hurt herself. She was too frightened to move, though, so she just lay there, eyes closed, pretending to be in a faint. She heard the man come through the bushes, stand hovering over her for a couple of seconds, then start running away.

So, as you can see, feigning a faint can be enough to stop the assault by itself. But even if it isn't, it has another virtue: it's a surprise for the rapist. He's expecting you to scream or struggle. By feigning a faint or going limp you've turned the tables somewhat. He now has to react. As a result, you have more time to think.

If going limp or pretending to faint isn't right for you,

for some reason or another—it isn't your style, the circumstances won't allow it (if, for instance, the assaulter has
come on only gradually, after a long conversation) or
you're just too scared to close your eyes, even for a little
while—then simply do nothing. *Nothing*. That alone won't
drive off an assaulter, but it will give you time to think.
Whenever you're in doubt during the assault, do nothing.
But don't stop thinking.

Let's say that's what you're doing right now, with the
assaulter clutching you in the bushes. He's trying to throw
you to the ground. You're trying to stay on your feet. What
do you do?

Don't wait for him to throw you to the ground, get down
there yourself. By doing that, you stop struggling to stay on
your feet (and we already know how the rapist feels about
any kind of struggling). And you remove the threat to him
that you'll try to run—and thereby lessen his need to
knock you senseless. Most important, by lying down, you
give the distinct impression that you're going to be submis-
sive.

Now, I'm not telling you to turn around every time
you're tapped on the shoulder and say, "Hey, wanna lie
down?" But in an assault, you've *helped* yourself by getting
on the ground, contrary to what you may have thought.
I've studied cases where women were all but killed on their
feet while struggling to keep from being thrown to the
ground.

For some reason, most women (and men, too) believe
that when they're thrown to the ground, all is lost. On the
contrary. The rapist has to get down there too. He doesn't
have artillery. He's not plastic man. And remember, an
assaulter's strength is his main weapon. Without leverage
and maneuverability, he can't use it effectively. On the
ground, his leverage and maneuverability will be cut in
half, compared to when he's standing. So, by getting on the

ground, you've actually evened the odds a bit against your assaulter, physically speaking.

Actually, you've done more, quite a bit more. You've gotten him close to you. This is what he wants, of course. But it's also what *you* want. The best techniques for foiling the assaulter are *not* dependent on leverage or maneuverability, but on proximity, on closeness.

You're almost always better off getting down on the ground when confronted with an assaulter, and accepting him down to you. The closer he gets to you, the more you can do to him—if necessary. He thinks he's got you, but he's wrong. As you will see, once you're both on the ground, it's just a matter of what you choose to do to him.

What you should be doing in these first moments of an assault is *analyzing* the situation. What does this man want from me? What is he prepared to do to me if he doesn't get what he wants? What resources do I have? What defenses can I use against him? Is there anything in the environment that helps me? Or hurts me? Or that I can use?

Now is the time to *use your imagination and your good judgment*. There you are, behind the bushes, lying on the ground, an assaulter about to leap on you and no help in sight. The only weapon you have is your mind. If it's functioning on all cylinders, it should be weapon enough.

If you use your imagination, you'll be able to come up with dozens of ways to turn the rapist away from you. In one case, a woman was grabbed by an assaulter while walking in a park and was flung to the ground. The assaulter then got down on top of her. "Now wait a moment," she told him. "I want what you want. But I can't have sex. I've got syphilis." She said she didn't even get a look at his face. The assaulter just leaped to his feet without a word and ran away, shaking his hands and brushing off his clothes.

Now, you might not be a good enough actress to carry that off. In that case, don't try it. But whatever you try, be sincere. I can just see someone half-heartedly trying to pull this off, and saying, "I've got syphilis," and he says, "Yeah, right, and I have gonorrhea. Let's trade."

If you're not totally convincing, the rapist will perceive you as insulting his intelligence. Which is the same as being antagonistic, and therefore very dangerous.

There are diseases other than syphilis that you might be more comfortable with. Maybe you've "just come back from the doctor" and he's told you you have mumps, measles, chickenpox, hepatitis, mononucleosis, rheumatic fever or something else that would encourage the rapist to look for some other woman. If one of these sounds natural to you, fine.

One woman I know of told the rapist she had cancer. "I said that if he raped me, he'd get it," she repeated to me. "He said he'd call my bluff—but he didn't. He ended up picking me up off the ground and even brushing off my coat. He said that he was sorry I had cancer. And he left."

John M. MacDonald, associate professor of psychiatry at the University of Colorado School of Medicine, in his book *Rape—Offenders and Their Victims* cites several similar cases. In one, a woman told her attacker that if he raped her she would kill herself. Evidently she was convincing. And evidently, he only wanted to rape her, not be responsible for her death. He ran off.

Another woman told her attacker that her mother had just died, and still another told her assaulter that she had a roommate who would be eager to have sex with him. Evidently neither man knew how to respond, and so departed quickly.

One woman who heard my lecture told me that she had been standing on a curb at noon, waiting for a bus, when a car pulled up and a man leaped out, pointed a gun at her head and said, "Come on, get in." She was very frightened.

"What sort of a person could have a gun pointed at his or her head and not be scared?" was what she told me. But her mind didn't stop working. She told the man, "I can't come with you, I'm in my period. I've just come from the gynecologist and I'm having serious discharge problems. I just can't do it now." The guy grabbed her by the hair and placed his hand on her breast—evidently to test her sincerity. She repeated that she would go with him but she couldn't do it, she was in her period. After what seemed like the longest time to her (it was probably less than a minute), he got back into his car and drove off. Perhaps he wasn't going to kill her anyway, but you'd never convince this woman of that.

She turned the tables on the man by surprising *him*. She said, in effect, I'm going to have to decline your invitation. He couldn't figure out a comeback, so he left.

MacDonald quotes a woman who tells a similar story:

"This man came up to me and grabbed me and said, 'Take off your dress.' And I said, 'Are you going to rape me? If you're planning to rape me, this isn't the right time.' He thought about this for a moment, then asked why. I said because it's right in the middle of my period. 'I'm having my flow. Do you know what happens whan you have intercourse with someone during this period? You get blistered.' He thought about this for a while, then released me . . ."

Most of these cases so far *do* demonstrate imagination— but only in talking your way out of assault. Imagination by actions, as opposed to talk, is a very good alternative, perhaps better than talking in some instances. The key is to communicate any way you can.

A South Carolina woman who had heard me speak told of a night when her date was driving her home from a movie. He stopped the car on a deserted side street and began insisting on "payment" for his trouble. Sound famil-

iar? Why some men think that women "owe" them in addition to their company is beyond me.

She said, "I tried every way possible to convince him
that I didn't want to make love. Not just to him, but to
anybody. I was careful to add that, because it kept buzzing
around in my head what you said about not being antagonistic. But nothing I said worked. He started tearing off my
blouse, then my pants. I did try to resist some—against
your suggestions, I know—but it didn't help. He was too
strong and he just got more excited.

"He then pulled me down on top of him and was attempting to penetrate me. All I could remember you saying
is: 'when with your date, if everything else fails, turn him
off. Do something weird if you have to. But turn him off.'
It's hard thinking in a situation like that. But over and over
again I kept hearing 'Turn him off,' 'Use your imagination,' 'Do something weird.' He was just about to penetrate
me. I was on top. Well, I urinated all over him. And you
know what? It turned him off.

"Then to make sure he didn't get mad, I told him that I
had chronic kidney problems, and when I got excited, I
couldn't control myself. Boy, was he embarrassed that he'd
put me through that. He apologized, and apologized, and
apologized."

So much for the myth of the helpless woman.

In another case I know of, a young woman was grabbed
by two men and thrown into the back seat of a car. One
hopped into the driver's seat and started driving the car
away, the other stayed in the back with the woman, tearing
her clothes off and beating her viciously.

"I wasn't struggling," she told me—she'd heard one of
my lectures before this happened—"but he didn't realize
that." (Can you see how a frightened man could easily
perceive as struggling a woman who is just avoiding his

blows? Remember, things *are* as they are *perceived* by the perceiver.) "I knew I had to convince him, so I grabbed one of his hands and placed it on my breast. He looked at me in astonishment, and I looked back with the best smile I could manage. He started stripping. Message received. Just as he got his pants down, the car pulled up to a red light. I opened the door and jumped out."

This woman told me that a lot of women probably couldn't do what she did. "But you know something," she said, "I really didn't want to be raped. And I would have done anything at all to prevent it."

Not every one of these methods will work every time. But none of them will leave you in worse shape than you were before, if they don't work. You'll always have a chance to try something else.

In one case I have on file, a woman got out of the assault situation by faking cramps. She doubled over, moaned and groaned and the rapist left her.

In another instance, a woman avoided rape by saying that she was three months pregnant—far enough along to be in a delicate condition, but not so far along that it showed. No one, not even a doctor, can tell at a glance whether a woman is three months pregnant. This woman simply told her assaulter not to lie on her stomach, to treat her gently, to take care because of the baby. He said he didn't want to hurt a little baby and took off.

There really is no end to what will work, to what can be thought up on the spur of the moment. When the Boston Strangler was on a rampage in the Boston area, one woman let him in, believing his claim that the superintendent had sent him to do some repairs on the toilet. Then, when he put his hands on her, she realized her danger. "Ssshhh," she whispered, smiling and winking, "my husband's asleep in the other room." The man left quickly.

The technique might not have worked if she'd said, "Take your hands off me or I'll call my husband." There was no husband there and the rapist might have called her bluff. But she faked complicity. That convinced him she was telling the truth.

Many a woman has turned away an assaulter with a variation of that ploy. "Moose is asleep, let's not make any noise." Or, "Ox doesn't like to be awakened, especially after his karate class. We'd better be quiet."

Vulgar and unfeminine behavior will often turn off a rapist as in the urination case above. Although I would limit these techniques to the situation of being raped by someone you *know* or to situations where you perceive the incident as a possible "pickup" (as with the two women who faked homosexuality), I have cases on file where a woman has avoided rape or injury by (1) picking her nose, (2) burping and belching, (3) scratching her behind, (4) urinating, (5) defecating or passing wind or some combination of these. If you've made yourself unattractive, unfeminine and vulgar, you've lessened your desirability. Now, some of these tactics are not very polite, but during an assault, the rules of etiquette are temporarily suspended. Anything is correct within the realm of your imagination if it works—or cannot harm you.

Outright weird behavior can also work. I know of one case where a woman, when attacked, dropped to all fours, started babbling insanely, ripping handfuls of grass out of the ground and began eating it. The attacker took one look at her and hightailed it out of there. He'd been shocked worse than she had.

Understand, she wasn't making cruel fun. She was trying to save herself from being raped. In my opinion, this woman used her imagination and took advantage of the resources she had. Her tactic worked because the rapist was searching for a normal available woman, not an escapee from an institution.

In another case I know of, a woman was asleep in one of those large, cross-country buses when a man plopped down beside her and put his hand on her breast. Remembering an animal-like karate cry I demonstrated in a lecture, she looked at him, contorted her face as much as possible, held up one hand, distorted it into a kind of claw, scratched herself under the arm with her other hand and screeched away. The guy pulled his hand away from her as if he'd been burned, looked at her as though she were crazy, jumped up from his seat and took refuge at the back of the bus. This woman had not only made herself unfeminine, but she'd also made herself inhuman.

As another example of this kind of improvised behavior, one woman held her breath and started to turn blue when she was attacked. The assaulter looked at her, worried, and asked what was wrong. "I . . . I've got a . . . a heart murmur," she said. He nodded and backed away from her, out of the area, out of her life. Now, she didn't have any heart murmur, but during the assault, she remembered that when she was younger she'd often scared her parents by holding her breath and turning blue.

In another case I have on file, a woman in her sixties got on a bus and a man got on behind her. The two of them sat down, side by side. The man, apparently a young executive, threw his overcoat over his lap and it just happened to land on hers. His hand just happened to come to rest on her thigh. He started to fondle her.

The woman later told me that she considered telling him off right away, but then she thought that he probably does this all the time. She decided to teach him a lesson. She waited several seconds until she could think of exactly the right thing to say. And finally she turned to him. "Sir," she said gently, "would you please be careful? You're going to unbuckle the strap—to my wooden leg." The man went into shock and actually fainted in his bus seat.

In another case, when a man leaped at a woman and began tearing at her blouse, she quickly unbuttoned and thrust her breasts out at him.

For a few seconds he gazed at her in astonishment and disbelief. Finally, he backed up and ran. She'd turned the tables on him, making him the victim of surprise rather than accepting that status herself. Evidently, when confronted with such a blatant but sincere invitation, the rapist's confidence—never great—shriveled up to nothing. This story illustrates that sometimes an invitation to sexual activity is just as likely to discourage a rapist as it is to entice him.

All of this behavior doesn't violate any of the basic laws of assault safety: it doesn't antagonize; it appears to be either involuntary or psychotic; it doesn't commit your behavior. You can always stop acting that way if you have to. Even if it doesn't work, it won't hurt you. It's not violent, it's not insulting. Through confidence in themselves these women were able to come up with a successful idea. And I'm convinced that there are dozens of similar ideas that no one has thought of yet.

You're limited only by your imagination. Remember where we were, earlier, with you in the bushes, about to be attacked? Well, picture yourself there for a moment. Are there any of these responses you could use? Have you a natural tendency you could easily exaggerate? Take a moment *now* and choose or invent a couple of ideas along these lines. Tuck them away in your mind somewhere where you can get to them if you need them. Make sure that what you've chosen is something within your character, something you can actually do.

Remember that this kind of behavior *might not work*.

You may not be able to carry it off, and even if you do, your assaulter may not be discouraged by it. Fortunately, gimmicks or weird behavior are only one approach to avoiding rape or mutilation, and by no means the strongest one.

5

A Lesson in Psychological Karate

Let's say now that you're back where you were, in the bushes, lying on the ground, and your assaulter is about to do whatever it is he plans to do. You've regained your emotional stability. You've used your imagination and good judgment. Maybe you've tried one of the tactics I've described, only to have it laughed off by your assaulter. He's pulled out a knife and told you you'd better do as he says. What now?

If you recall, we have three principles we haven't touched on yet, at least not directly: (1) *treat the rapist as a human being*, (2) *gain his confidence*, (3) *go along until you can safely react*. You're going to have to use them now.

Before you can practice any of these principles, however, you have to *establish communication* with the man. You have to set up a hot line to your assaulter and start using it. Communication is so important, it could actually be our sixth principle, except that it's an integral part of all the others.

The medium doesn't have to be words. Some assaulters have only contempt for small talk. You'll know soon enough if the man who's attacked you feels this way. He'll say, "Shut up." There are other communication mediums available to you, however: smiles, gestures, touches, glances, the entire range of body language.

But words are by far the best way to communicate with your assaulter, if he'll allow them. Many times a woman has avoided rape and injury by engaging the rapist in a lengthy conversation, where the talk became so intimate it was, in effect, therapy. Occasionally, these conversations have lasted for hours, ending with the rapist's departure before he did anything more serious to his victim than speak to her.

In a way, such a conversation is simply one long period of stalling. More important, it is the means to treat the rapist as a human being and to gain his confidence. That in itself may be sufficient to cause him to break off his attack.

Okay, let's get back to our little drama in the park. "What do you want," you say, initiating conversation. "Lie still," he replies, "you'll find out soon enough."

This is the time you should concentrate on treating him as a human being and on gaining his confidence, so that you will have an opportunity to create a moment during which you can safely react and get out of the assault.

The first step is to convince your attacker that you're *not* what he thinks you are, just one more snotty woman who believes she's better than he is.

Earlier, I told you to get on the ground if that's where your assaulter wants you, and to get there *before* he's forced to put you there himself. Now I'm saying that you should act humble in his presence and that you should demonstrate this humility as quickly and as clearly as you can, *before* he's forced to humiliate you himself. You're dealing with a man who is angry at women in large part because he thinks they're better than he is or he thinks *they* think they are better than he is. You'll greatly reduce his anger and his need to degrade you if you can convince him that you, for one, are not aloof and arrogant and contemptuous of him or repelled by what is happening.

That won't be your natural inclination. When you're grabbed, you'll understandably want to say something like, "Get your hands off me, you disgusting animal." Even though your feelings are perfectly justified, I don't think I have to tell you that's asking for trouble even when you're dealing with your husband or boyfriend.

Even if you're able to take on an attitude of humility, it won't be easy to convey that to your assaulter. Even if you *don't* call him names, or shy away from his touch as if he were a leper, or look at him as if he's the lowest scum on the face of the earth, he may perceive you as doing just that. His life experiences have conditioned him to believe women react to him negatively, no matter how they actually feel or what they say.

A man like this will see you as being arrogant and contemptuous if you're merely acting naturally. If you act humble, he'll see you as acting naturally. Only if you're superhumble will he begin to get the message you're trying to convey.

The only way you can convince this man that you don't consider yourself better than he is is to exaggerate your humility, to overplay your hand. Only when you do that will he feel he's been accorded respect and been treated as a human being.

It's not an easy task to be humble when you're about to be raped, but one approach is to let your motherly instincts come out. Whatever threat he may pose to you, remember that a rapist is a man in trouble, a man who needs help as simple and, by the way, as precious, as empathy from another human being. Dwell on that.

Dr. MacDonald cites a case in which a woman in her middle fifties got into a taxi, only to be followed in by an assaulter with a gun, who immediately ordered the cabbie to drive off.

"He kept saying he was going to kill me," the woman said. "I was crying and pleading with him for our lives and this was just making him more violent. Finally, I decided our only hope was for me to go along with him. So I told him he reminded me of my own son. I told him . . . we could go to my apartment. Then he was completely different, apologizing and saying he was sorry."

The taxi driver added these remarks:

"The woman had plenty of sense and plenty of guts. She started telling him she liked him and . . . I think this is what got us out alive, because as long as she was crying and screaming, he just got worse and worse. But once she started talking to him, he calmed down, he was entirely different."

At first, this woman made mistakes. It's very likely you will too. But, as you can see, it's what you do after you make the initial mistakes that counts, providing the initial mistake doesn't last too long. In this case, the woman did her best to treat the rapist as a human being. She acted with exaggerated friendliness, saying that he reminded her of her own son. And it worked.

Another approach to humility is to portray yourself as feeling low, and being on no one's pedestal. You can turn to your assaulter and say, "You know, I was feeling so lonely tonight. I was half hoping someone would come along." Or, "I really needed to meet someone tonight. It was just luck that *you* came by." Or, "I was so scared, until I saw you."

Besides conveying humility, this tactic forces on the assaulter an unexpected assumption: that this is a social situation, not an assault, and that the normal social rules therefore apply. By your response, you've announced your expectations of him and they're not the expectations a victim has of her rapist. This is *very* important.

Still another approach is to be just as warm and human as you can be—kind, thoughtful, empathetic, respectful, sweet, even loving, in the broad sense. The surest way to do this is to find the good in your attacker and show him you can acknowledge it. Comment on his looks, his strength, his clothing, his build, his intelligence, his hair, his shoes, his cleverness, his car, his voice, his anything good. There will be *something* good about him, I guarantee it. Showing him that you acknowledge that, expressing your admiration, has two effects: it automatically puts you into a position of humility and it helps him see *himself* in a different light.

The next step in treating the assaulter as a human being is to convince him that *he* isn't what he thinks he is. He starts out seeing himself as pretty low on the totem pole. More than most of the rest of us, he needs to feel good about himself. If you help him toward that feeling, you're not only getting off the pedestal he's put you on, you're also raising his image of himself.

Many woman have successfully used such remarks as, "You're too good-looking to be doing this . . ." or "I'll bet you can get any girl you want, anyway." Like everyone else, rapists like to hear compliments. And, like everyone else, they want to believe the nice things they hear about themselves. They are people, after all.

In one case in my files, a woman was walking home from the office. It was dusk and a man was following her. When she realized that she was being tailed, she speeded up. So did her follower. She didn't know whether to run or scream or turn around and start fighting.

About fifty steps from her apartment, with her follower rapidly closing the gap, she got an idea. She turned and looked directly at him. "Mister," she said, "I've been followed home from work every night this week"—which wasn't true—"and I'm scared to death"—which was. "Would you please mind walking me to my apartment?"

She then put her arm in his, making no effort to disguise her fear. By her actions, she was showing him that she trusted him. It was someone else she was worried about.

The man hesitated for a moment. "Well," he said finally, "sure. I'd be happy to."

He walked her up to her door and she handed him her key. He unlocked the door, opened it for her, then handed her back the key. "Thank you," she said with a smile. She walked in, closed the door, locked it—and called the police, giving them the man's description.

Several hours later they picked him up. As it turned out, he had a past record of molesting women, though he'd never been convicted of rape.

Without knowing exactly why she had acted this way, this woman had done exactly the right thing. She had given the man a great deal of ego enhancement. The way most men think, there is no better way for a man to prove he *is* a man, to himself, than protecting a young woman in distress. Can you think of a more convincing way to treat an assaulter as a human being than to ask him for help?

In another case I have personal knowledge of, a woman was at a college dance. She walked out of the building to get a breath of fresh air and was accosted almost immediately by a strange man, who grabbed her. She was momentarily startled, but quickly regained her wits.

"Weren't you at the dance?" she asked. She was fairly sure she'd seen him inside.

"Ah, well, ah, yes," her assaulter replied.

The woman smiled at him seductively. "I followed you out here," she confided.

"You did?" The assaulter was surprised and pleased, too taken aback to be skeptical.

"That's right," the woman said. "I was hoping you'd talk to me. That dance was deadly dull. Would you like to go someplace with me where we could, you know, be alone?"

"Would I? You bet I would!"

"Great. Now you go get your car while I go back and tell my roommate I'm going to be late tonight." She pressed her body against him and gave him a quick kiss on the cheek. Then she turned and went back into the hall. The last she saw of her assaulter, he was hurrying to get his car.

The moment she stepped back into the auditorium, the woman screamed bloody murder. No problem—her attacker couldn't hurt her there. This is probably the only circumstance when you can safely scream—when you *know* you can get to help. You can't count on it getting to you. At any rate, the campus security men scoured the area and finally apprehended the man, an ex-student, by the way. But there was nothing they could do to him—because *he* hadn't done anything. The woman's imaginative handling of the situation ended the assault before it really got underway.

Take note that each of the tactics the women in these cases used were appropriate to the particular environment. Remember, the environment is one of the assault variables and you must not omit it in your evaluation.

In another instance, a woman saved herself by using the rapist's real need for acceptance. Her assaulter had thrown her to the ground. She lay there dazed for a moment, collecting her wits, and said, "Listen, I've always wanted to have normal sex with someone. But I've always been so afraid of what happened to me when I was seven years old. My stepfather raped me. So please, please be gentle with me, make it good for me."

The rapist stopped hitting her and listened. "Your stepfather?" he said. "That's disgusting. And you were only seven years old?"

"Yes. And my doctor says that the reason I've never been able to . . . well, you understand."

"Yeah," the assaulter said. He seemed stymied. "Hey," he said at last, "you get up and get out of here. And don't walk through parks like this alone. That's stupid."

The woman did as she was told, went home and called the police.

By asking her assaulter to be gentle, she had paid him the supreme compliment. The implication was that though no man had been able to make sex satisfying to her in the past, she hoped and believed that he could.

Treating the rapist as a human being, by changing *both* his perception of you and his perception of himself, can sometimes nullify an attack almost before it begins. But often that by itself is not enough. You must also concentrate on gaining your assaulter's confidence by convincing him that you pose no threat to him whatever. Many times, this will flow naturally if you simply treat him as a human being. The woman at the dance who promised her assaulter she'd go off with him certainly gained his confidence. So did the woman who handed her apartment key to the man who'd been following her. But it isn't enough that gaining the rapist's confidence comes as a by-product. It's something you should concentrate on, especially if your assaulter has a weapon.

Dr. MacDonald quotes one married woman who was assaulted by a man with a gun. He apparently told her he was going to rape her, then kill her, so she couldn't identify him. Terrified, the woman submitted to him. Afterward, to quote her: "I started to cry. Then I realized that would scare him and I quickly told him, 'I'm all right. But I'm embarrassed. What will I tell my husband? It's so embarrassing I don't want anyone to catch you. I know you'll get away.' He raised the gun at me. I felt he was contemplating finishing me off. Then he ran."

Since this rapist was never caught, it's impossible to know for sure how he reacted to the woman's words. But it's a good bet that he believed her, that she gave him a reason not to kill her. The woman was raped, but because she gained the man's confidence, she's alive to tell about it.

In a case that comes out of my files, a woman in her late teens was attacked by a man who broke into her house by jimmying a door lock. The woman's parents weren't home, but her fifteen-year-old sister was asleep in a third-floor room, directly above the victim's. The assaulter came into her room, brandishing a butcher knife he'd evidently picked up in the kitchen. He put the knife to her throat, stripped her and told her to submit or he'd kill her. Though the girl had been rudely awakened, she managed to keep her cool. She didn't argue for a moment. Instead, she said, "Let me put in some Vaseline—that will make it easier." She knew he was tense and that struggling would be very dangerous, and she didn't want to be hurt.

By talking loudly and dropping things, she hoped to rouse her sister. And this is exactly what happened. Her sister heard her, got dressed, climbed down a tree near her window and got the police. By the time they arrived, the rapist had put his knife aside and was getting down to the business he came for. He was arrested, not on a rape charge but on the charges of breaking and entering and of assault with a deadly weapon—a verdict I find barbaric.

Several months after one of the first lectures I'd ever given, a seventeen-year-old woman who'd heard the lecture awoke at six-thirty on a Sunday morning in her dormitory, at a women's college in North Carolina, to find a naked man standing beside her bed, a handkerchief stretched between his hands. She was startled at first—who wouldn't be?—and she had to fight for her emotional stability. But she soon began talking to him.

"How did you get into the room?" she asked him.

"I climbed through the window," he said.

They kept talking for a while, about how difficult it had been for him to find a way to open the window, how he'd managed to slip in quietly. According to what she told me, the woman began to realize that if anything, he was more nervous than she was. Finally, she said, "Do you mind if I go to the bathroom and get a drink of water first?" Note the word "first." It clearly implied that something else was to follow. The woman was making a kind of promise, as had the woman at the dance.

"No," the man said, "I don't mind."

She got up out of bed and walked out of the room. Suddenly, the man was at the door, evidently checking to see if she was running. Very wisely, she wasn't. "I'll be right back," she said.

"Okay," he said. He went back into her room and closed the door.

The young woman proceeded straight past the women's room, down the hall, to the housemother, who promptly called the police. Before the police arrived, the woman and the housemother heard a noise, and through a window, saw the man running away.

There was no arrest, no prosecution—and for that matter, no assault. And all because this brilliant young woman handled the situation perfectly. First of all, she remained calm. Then she established communication with her assaulter by starting a conversation. During this conversation she treated the assaulter as a human being, not as an animal or a monster. The conversation helped to ease the tension in the situation and made violence much less likely. Then by saying she wanted to go to the bathroom "first," she was, in effect, saying, "Anything you want to do is fine—after I finish with the bathroom." This had the very definite effect of gaining the man's confidence. Finally, she did not run. She waited to react until she was sure she was safe.

It might not have turned out this well. Suppose the woman had screamed when she woke up and saw the intruder. He probably would have gagged her, at the very least. No doubt, that's why he was holding that handkerchief between his hands. Her screams probably wouldn't have been heard, since there was no one else on that floor of the dormitory except the housemother, who was way down the hall. And by screaming she probably would have ended up at the mercy of the assaulter. If she'd struggled she might have been beaten, injured—or murdered.

There are a few other words of caution. Keep in mind that if your assaulter is of an ethnic group that has been discriminated against, you have a very special problem in convincing him you're treating him as a human being. Because he has been discriminated against, he will tend to see you as prejudiced, even if, for example, both you and he are black. For that reason, you'll have to work that much harder to project humility. Look for the good, look for the person, try to reach him, not the stereotype. I want to emphasize, though, that situations of rape across racial lines are the exception. Amir's Philadelphia study showed that 93 percent of all rapes were carried out by black men against black women or white men against white women. Only 4 percent were white men against black women, and only 3 percent were black men against white women. Even so, there is an awful lot of racial fear mixed up with fear of rape. The important thing to remember is that if you cringe at the touch of someone of another ethnic group—and convey that repugnance to a potential assaulter—you're in trouble.

Another warning: make sure your assaulter doesn't perceive your remarks as manipulative. If he thinks you're saying nice things to him solely to get him to take his hands off you, you're again in trouble. You must be convincing. For that reason, especially, you have to choose behavior that suits your personality and the environmental setting. You should be comfortable with the things you say or do; they should come naturally. When you look for the good in him, don't fake it. Find the *real* good. It's there. The rapist is a human being, and no human being is all bad.

You may well ask at this point, "Why does the rapist deserve such consideration? Why should I go out of my way to treat him as a human being, to act humble or to build up his ego?" If you've been asking yourself these questions, let me remind you that you don't want to be raped or mutilated or killed. If you can escape that fate by being considerate, by acting humble, by looking for the good in the rapist, the only wounds you may suffer will be to your dignity. Those will heal quickly, without scars. On second thought, would there really be any wounds at all?

6

If All Else Fails

My research shows that very nearly every woman who has acted in accord with all the recommendations we've discussed has neither been killed nor injured. The vast majority haven't been raped. And those who were *chose* rape as the lesser of two evils.

Though exceptions are almost nonexistent, there *are* exceptions, even among the women who do everything right. When women do everything right psychologically and still have troubles, the fault isn't theirs. Some rapists and assaulters are so emotionally disturbed that they *must* discharge their aggressions, no matter how skillfully the victim tries to defuse the situation. In some situations both the rapist and the woman get caught in the whirlpool of an event and the environment dictates the outcome.

And so, even women who behave intelligently are occasionally raped, or mutilated, or even sometimes murdered. That *needn't* happen. Beyond the psychological tactics we've talked about so far, there are several methods of self-defense that can prevent any or all of these consequences.

Any woman can use them, whether she's Wonderwoman or Tinkerbelle, against any assaulter, whether he's built like Atlas or Tweety-Bird, and whether the assault occurs in the lavatory of a 747, thirty-five thousand feet over the Atlantic, in an open meadow in Kansas with not another soul within ten miles, or a back alley in a big-city ghetto.

These methods aren't fun and games. They involve several ways to meet force with more force. *For that reason these techniques are not to be used unless all else has failed and only if you must act in immediate defense of your life or against severe bodily harm.*

I want to be very precise about "immediate defense of your life or severe bodily harm." I mean that within the *next three or four seconds* your assaulter will attempt to kill or badly injure you. I mean that if he is aiming his gun and he is about to squeeze the trigger. That he is thrusting his knife your way. That he is swinging a club or chain at you. That he is choking you and you're dying. That he is clubbing you with his fists or hitting you with all his might in an effort to kill or injure you—not just slapping you around or punching you a few times so you'll stop struggling. (Depending on a woman's attitude, and on whether or not penetration is accompanied by a beating and/or threats of injury or death, rape could be considered severe bodily harm.) I mean that you are about to be tied up by your assaulter. This is essentially the same as being in immediate danger of your life or severe bodily harm, since it puts you in the position of total jeopardy. From the moment you are tied up, your life and well-being continue only at the mercy of your assailant. And since he is emotionally disturbed, his actions are entirely unpredictable.

If you doubt that you must act in immediate defense of your life or against severe bodily harm when you are about to be tied up, just remember what happened to those seven nurses in Chicago a few years ago. Richard Speck told them he wasn't going to hurt them, that he just wanted to make sure they didn't run away. They let him tie them up and he murdered them one by one. The two killers in Truman Capote's superb *In Cold Blood* also tied up their victims before killing them.

Now that we've defined "immediate defense of your life or severe bodily harm," let's examine what it *doesn't* mean.

You're not in this situation if:

You're grabbed by the hair and pulled or shoved to the ground.

Your assaulter puts a knife to your throat. This is just a threat—so far. If he wanted to kill you, he'd slash your throat and get it over with, without conversation. Unfortunately, many women react as if their lives are in immediate danger when they're threatened this way—which isn't surprising. As a result, many struggle violently and *cut their own necks*, by accident. This sometimes happens even when the assaulter intends no violence. (Probably more often than just sometimes.)

A man points a gun at you and commands you to do one thing or another "or else." (Again, you're faced with a threat, not an immediate attack on your life.)

Your assaulter socks you and growls out something about killing you. (Once more, he's only threatening. You may have to turn off this threat by using your wits, but you're certainly *not* in *immediate* danger of your life or severe bodily harm.)

Your assaulter seems almost ready to use a weapon, though he's not using it yet. If the actual attack on your life is *five to ten seconds* away or longer, you're not in *immediate* danger, by the definition I'm giving. You can still change the situation.

It's easy enough to make the definition clear in a book, but in the event of an assault, your inclination will be to instantly assume you're in immediate danger of your life or severe bodily harm. That's one of the effects of a surprise attack. Just remember this: if you can ask yourself, "Am I in immediate danger of my life or severe bodily harm?" you're probably *not*. If you have time to ask yourself the question, you also have time to change the situation, to deal with the assault in ways I've already described.

Remember also that only rarely—compared with the total number of rapes and assaults—are women mutilated in assaults, and almost never murdered. You'll probably never be in immediate danger of your life even if you are assaulted. In the unlikely event that you are, the danger will almost never come at the beginning of an assault, before you've had a chance to think. It will come later on, after you've regained some measure of emotional stability. And, with a reasonable amount of emotional stability, and the technique we're going to discuss, you'll not only be able to save your own life, you'll be able to *do away* with your assaulter, if necessary and if you so choose.

Some of the following self-defense techniques can be deadly to the assaulter if you go far enough with them. That's why it's necessary to be precise about defining when they should be used. It's a matter of law, the law of self-defense. This law varies somewhat from state to state, but, at the minimum, it denies you the right to take human life in defense of property and allows you to take human life in defense of your life or in defense against severe bodily harm—provided you have exhausted all other possibilities.

"All right," you say, "so the law allows me to kill the guy, to defend myself. But I'm not even sure I can make him wince, much less kill him."

Let me assure you that you *can* hurt him. With almost no effort on your part, you can hurt him so badly he will give up the assault instantly, lose all interest in you, and go into shock. With very little more, you can do away with him, permanently. All you have to do is get him into the right position. Chances are, he'll be there already, if you use all of the principles we're talking about. In addition, the very nature of his attack will usually put him in the right position.

There's only one preparatory step: get close to your assaulter. Many woman feel that they should keep as great a distance from him as possible. That's wrong. The assaulter who carries a weapon or depends on his strength will be able to use one or the other more effectively at arm's length. The best self-defense methods are useful only at short range. That's where he'll be, sooner or later, or how else can he rape?

Getting as close to you as possible will usually be among the rapist's prime goals. But if the man who has assaulted you seems interested more in violence than anything else, if he seems perfectly happy to stand a few steps from you and use a weapon on you, before you do anything to him you have to get him close to you. How? By turning his attack into a sexual assault. Use sex as a weapon if you must. Encourage him to put his hands on sexual areas of your body. Or put them there yourself if you have to. Or put your hands on him. Offer yourself to him. Make sexual overtures. And be sure you're convincing. He may not change his mind about killing you, but he'll certainly think of something he'd like to do first.

The same goes for the assaulter who wants to tie you up. Once you're tied up, there's no way you can get close to him of your own free will. But while he's getting out the rope or making the knots you still have an opportunity. Tell him, show him, if necessary, that you can make it better for him if you're able to move your hands and your body. Come on strong, sexually. If he wants to tie you up, say, "Sure, why not? Later, though. I have a better idea for now." And I'll tell you one thing: you'll be a lot more able to handle sex than violence. After all, if he touches your breast, you'll still be able to think clearly. But if he's smashing you in the face with his fist—well, you choose.

So—there in the bushes—your assaulter was about to stab you, you sacrificed your dignity, ignored your moral code for the moment, reached up and placed his hand on your breast. He looked at you quizzically for a moment. You smiled. He smiled back, put his knife away, and pushed up close to you, perhaps partially disrobing both of you first. You have every reason to believe that after he's raped you, the knife will reappear and you will be in danger of your life. What do you do?

You affectionately place your hands on the sides of your assaulter's face, gently putting them exactly where you would if you were going to tenderly pull his face toward yours for a kiss. Then you put both thumbs over his eyes and press, about as hard as if you were attempting to slip your thumbs into a jar of preserves. If he is wearing eyeglasses, you'll find you can easily slip your thumbs beneath them. If he's wearing contacts, it won't matter.

What you're doing, if you haven't guessed, is putting your assaulter's eyes out, actually pushing your thumbs into his eyesockets. Press hard enough and the eyes will be shoved back against his cortex killing him. At the very least, he will go into shock and pass out. He may be temporarily blinded. He may be permanently blinded. Not nice, you say? I agree, but you have the right to defend yourself any way you can if you're in immediate danger of your life or severe bodily harm. It's you—or him.

Half the women who read this advice would never be able to put out someone's eyes no matter what was done to them. And the other half probably couldn't wait to get to him, if they're assaulted. It's impossible for anyone to tell you that you *should* do such a thing. What you do depends on your own attitude, values and morals, your personal frame of reference. You can learn the means to defend yourself, if it comes to that. But only you can choose whether or not to use it.

Putting out someone's eyes is a pretty gruesome business, and it may be disgusting even to consider it. But remember, it isn't much compared with what some assaulters have done to some women. The gang rape of an eleven-year-old girl is worse than disgusting. The eye technique is mild by comparison. But it would serve no purpose to describe the gory details of assault cases; the news media takes care of this for us all too well.

The technique I have just given you differs from the self-defense techniques I've dismissed in earlier chapters in that it will work every single time. And it won't commit your behavior until *after* you're finished finishing him. It will work wherever you are, lying down or standing up, regardless of how weak you may be or how strong he is. No matter how well built your assaulter is, he can't develop muscles over his eyeballs, and if he could he couldn't see you to find you. Either way, we've got him.

This is, without doubt, the best defensive tactic available to you if you are in immediate danger of your life or severe bodily harm. All you need remember is to be gentle and tender until the very last moment. That way, if you cannot go through with it, all you have to do is remove your hand and your assaulter is none the wiser. There is absolutely *no* way to miss. You are placing your hands delicately on his face and carefully laying your thumbs on his eyes—not taking a flying leap at him or stabbing or poking at his eyes from arm's length, so that you end up hitting him on the forehead or cheek or nose. That would do no good and it would irrevocably commit your behavior.

For the next best technique, the gentle approach is also the key. All you have to do is reach down slowly and carefully to your assaulter's testicles, tenderly place your hand on one of them, and, suddenly, without warning, squeeze. Hard. The testicles are about the same consistency and strength as a ripe plum—without the pit. Any woman can squeeze one flat in a single motion.

One squeeze will send your assaulter into instant shock. If he is standing he will fall to the ground. If he is conscious he will be in excruciating pain, moaning, unable to rise. If he is lying down he will go limp. During a lecture, a woman interrupted while I was describing this technique and asked, "Won't he get mad?" Yes, he will get mad, but he won't be able to do anything.

A man describing to a woman how sensitive to pain the testicles are has no easy task, since there is no comparable area on a woman's body. The testicles are internal organs that nature has placed outside the body, since sperm, which the testicles produce, can't live at 98.6°F. They're protected only by a thin sac of skin, the scrotum, and to some extent, by their placement (the penis, which is quite insensitive to pain, hangs in front of the testicles).

Even a light flick to the testicles with your finger can send a momentarily incapacitating shock of pain through a man's system, cramping his body, forcing him to double over. Most of the time when you see a football player lying disabled on the field, he hasn't "had the wind knocked out of him," he's just gotten a knock on the testicles. And that despite the special protective cup he wears—and only a knock, not a smash.

Of course, every man knows his testicles are vulnerable. Including the rapist. That's why he's likely to react violently if you try to kick him or knee him in the groin. Why then would he let you actually squash one of his testicles?

The reason is sexual—combined with the element of surprise. Hitting the testicles hurts like hell, but when they're fondled, the result is sexual pleasure, excitation and anticipation. I have a number of cases on file where an assaulter has actually *ordered* his victim to fondle his testicles, putting her in the position of incapacitating him, if only she had the knowledge. The Boston Strangler did this in at least one case. Even the assaulter who doesn't order you to fondle him there will perceive that you are going along if you gently touch that area. He'll view it as a cooperation, not antagonism.

Let me emphasize that you should place your hand very gently, very tenderly on your assaulter's testicles. Your aim is to convince him that you're out to do him good, not harm. If you haven't struggled or screamed, especially if you haven't attempted to kick him, he won't be suspicious. In fact, he'll probably take down his trousers for you so that you can get to his testicles more easily. But it doesn't matter if he doesn't—the tactic is just as effective when the man's trousers are on, so long as you wait until you are *actually* cupping one of the testicles before you squeeze.

Like the eye push, the testicle squeeze will always work. Like the eye push, there's no way the assaulter will perceive the testicle squeeze as antagonistic, until it's too late for him. And as with the eye push, if you find that you cannot do it, all you have to do is remove your hand and he'll never know what you were considering. He may even ask you to put it back, so you'll have a second chance.

The key to both the testicle squeeze and the eye push is gentleness—until the actual moment the technique is used. Gentleness lets you get so close to the vulnerable part that you can't miss. Gentleness prevents the assaulter from thinking you're trying to harm him. Gentleness defuses his aggression. This alone makes it worthwhile. If you are violent instead of gentle, if you try to kick or knee your assaulter in the groin, if you try to jab out his eyes, your chances of missing skyrocket, since you're striking from a distance.

By the way, the testicle squeeze is particularly useful if

you're grabbed from behind and your arms are pinned to your sides. No matter how tightly you're grasped, all you have to do is move your hips slightly from side to side, then very, very gently reach back to his testicles and do away with your assailant. The tactic is also especially effective if you've already been penetrated. Suppose you've decided to allow penetration, then during the act your assaulter indicates or you perceive he'll hurt or kill you anyway. In that case, the best moment for the testicle squeeze is when he is approaching his climax, or during it. The assaulter has other things on his mind at that instant. He'll never be more helpless. And after you squeeze, he won't be anxious to do a song and dance.

The eye push and the testicle smash are the first and second best methods of self-defense during the rape situation. They are nearly equal in effectiveness and they are always available. These are the *only* two techniques that I can advocate without reservation. But there are others that can be useful in specific situations or if you are for one reason or another unwilling or unable to use one of the two techniques I recommend. Note, however, that the following self-defense techniques are at best *very poor alternatives.*

Now, let us proceed to method No. 427—there is nothing in between. Gently put your hands on the sides of your assaulter's face, the same position as the eye push, with your palms on his cheeks. Then, reach back behind his ears, slightly, under his earlobes, to where the jawbone and the skull meet, and push up with your index fingers. Between the end of the jawbone and the skull there is a small opening in the bony structure that is filled with nerve endings. Nerve endings are the unspecialized receptors of pain. Press your index fingers up into these two openings (they're just below the skin) and hold firmly for two or three seconds. Your assaulter will usually pass out and go into shock. If you hold on for six seconds, he may possibly die from the shock.

It's not because you might kill him that I rate the under-earlobe hold a distant 427th to the eye push and the testicle squeeze. Remember, we're fighting force with force here. We're talking about methods to be used when you are in immediate danger of your life or of severe bodily harm, when all else has failed. The reason this method ranks lower than the other two is that the area is rather small, about the size of a nickel, and there's always the chance you won't be able to find it or be able to have two seconds or longer to utilize it.

If you can't find the sensitive under-earlobe area, your assaulter won't know what you had in mind if you're gentle. You can then try one of the other techniques I've suggested. The assaulter won't become suspicious of you putting your hands on his cheeks, since that kind of gesture is common as a prelude to kissing.

There are still other methods that can, but don't always, incapacitate an attacker. Nowhere near comparable with the testicle and eye techniques, these rank somewhere near the earlobe method. I refer to tongue biting or lip biting. If you bite down hard enough on either of these areas of your attacker's body, drawing blood, you may incapacitate him.

This technique was invented, on the spot, *in extremis*, by a woman who'd heard one of my lectures and later reported her success to me.

Vicki had returned to her room one day and opened her closet door. A man jumped out at her, his arms flailing wildly, beating at her savagely, throwing her against the furniture and the walls.

"Throughout the beating, the confusion and the terror," she later told me, "I remembered from your lecture that 'if you don't know what to do, don't do anything—go limp—

become inanimate, lifeless.' So I went limp, on the floor. He suddenly stopped beating me and came down on top of me and began forcefully kissing me."

"He must have thought you were struggling," I said.

"Well, maybe—a little. Even though I know you said not to," she confessed.

"I also said that everyone makes mistakes in that sort of situation, if you remember. The important thing is, you reversed your mistakes. You regained your emotional stability and took rational action. What happened next?"

She told me that even though she'd stopped struggling, he made it clear—by words or actions—that he intended to kill her. So taking advantage of his nearness, she put her hands on his face and tried to prepare herself to put out his eyes.

She couldn't do it. And when she realized that, she knew she had to come up with something else. "I remembered something else you said in your lecture," she told me. "When you talked about kissing, you said that the upper lip was very, very sensitive. Well, I opened my mouth and clamped my teeth down on his upper lip with all the strength I had. I bit it—almost all the way off."

Vicki's assaulter went into shock instantly and passed out.

Faced with what she perceived as an immediate threat to her life, she took strong, positive action—and it worked. She took a risk, of course, but she took a *calculated* risk. She didn't simply lash out blindly. She thought about what she should do. She took rational action. She used her imagination. She showed good judgment.

Every time I describe these physical methods of self-defense in a lecture, a woman asks, "What if the assaulter is choking you and he is holding you at arm's length and his arms are so long that you can't reach his eyes or testicles?"

The assaulter gets most of his sexual satiation from holding the woman's body against his own. Further, he feels more secure about controlling you when he holds you close to him. So he doesn't want to be holding you at arm's length. But in the unlikely event that you experience such an assault, here's what to do.

Grasp one of his fingers, preferably the pinky, with both of your hands and let your weight go out from under you immediately and completely. This will cause a dislocated fracture of his finger, and severe pain. Don't grasp his whole *hand*, because your weight won't be enough to do any damage there.

This technique definitely is not as good as the eye push, the testicle smash or even the under-earlobe hold, since if the man is angry or excited enough, a dislocated finger, painful as it is, may not be incapacitating. Many men have played an entire game of professional hockey with injuries far worse than that, and no one has ever managed such a feat with a smashed testicle or a pushed-out eye.

For this reason, I do *not* advocate the finger pull, except in the single instance in which you are being held at arm's length and being choked, and cannot reach the man's eyes or testicles, and cannot turn the attack into a sexual assault. Even then, you might try just going limp first. Only use this technique if you feel you're being choked to death and *have to* do something. This will be perceived as struggling. And remember, struggling works only 50 percent of the time.

Women also ask me what to do if the assaulter is coming at them at a run, swinging a chain or a club or some other weapon, where going along until you see a chance to safely react is out of the question. Another physical self-defense technique is useful in that situation, though *only* in that situation. It is known as the front thrust kick and it's part of *sho-do-kan* karate.

With a front thrust kick, you can deliver a blow nearly eleven times as powerful as you can with your fist. Directed at your assaulter's kneecap, it can be frightfully disabling. The kneecap is extremely fragile. It is held in place by ligaments which are also fragile. If you connect with a front thrust kick against an assaulter's kneecap, you won't kill him, you probably won't even put him into shock. But you *will* be able to walk away from him faster than he can crawl. And crawling will be his *only* means of locomotion.

The front thrust kick is simple to learn, though you'll have to practice it several dozen times to get it right. First, stand flatfooted on both feet. Then, bring the knee of one leg up sharply at least parallel to the floor and swing the lower portion of your leg, your calf, straight out with a snap, keeping your instep up and aiming to make an impact with *only* your heel. (And it doesn't matter whether you're wearing gym shoes or high heels. Remember, karateists use the kick effectively with nothing more than bare feet.) After the impact, bring your lower leg back quickly and then down to a standing position.

The whole thing has to be done with snap. If you do it slowly, or if you merely paw at your assaulter with your foot, he may be able to catch your leg and pull you down. If you do it with a snap, the only thing he'll be able to catch is some broken bones in his hand and forearm—if he's dumb enough to reach for you.

Don't use this *except* in a situation where the assaulter is coming at you, and therefore exposing his knees with each step. This technique, valuable as it is, shouldn't be used unless you are in immediate danger of your life or severe bodily harm, *and* you perceive that you have no chance to survive by going along until a safer time. If you use this kick at the wrong time, or ineffectively, it can be very, very dangerous.

Still another physical self-defense technique, the wrist

release, could prove useful if you are in one particular situation: when someone grabs you by the wrist reaching out of his car or from a dark doorway, or from some bushes, and *safety is very near* (in the form of other people, open stores, etc.) Used in any other situation, the wrist release I'm about to describe is the same as struggling, with all of the associated risks and penalties.

When a man grabs you by the wrist, he holds you on one side with his four fingers, on the other with his thumb. Even if he is much stronger than you are, you can break his grip fairly easily by moving your arm and forearm *against the base of his thumb*, smartly. This point is the weakest part of the hand, the weakest joint in the body. If you push hard enough, you'll dislocate his thumb. What it amounts to is pitting your entire forearm and wrist against his thumb. If you concentrate your power on this motion and do it quickly, you'll break free.

A word of caution is also in order here: getting out of a wrist grab this way may mean going against your natural inclinations. When a person is grabbed by the wrist, the reaction is to attempt to pull away by pulling *back*. Depending on the position of your attacker's hand, that may be the wrong direction. You may be pushing against his four fingers, not his thumb. So to execute this technique properly, you may have to push away from your body *toward* him.

The key is the position of your attacker's thumb. Just remember to jerk quickly *against* his thumb with your entire forearm, whatever the position of his thumb on your wrist.

Get a friend to practice with you for a few moments. Have your friend grab your wrist, first from above, then from below, then from the side. Note the position of the thumb. Twist your wrist and forearm against it quickly.

(But take it easy when practicing—remember, you can dislocate your attacker's thumb this way.)

Remember, this technique will not incapacitate your attacker. It's only good when safety is a few steps away. But in this specific situation, it has been successfully used by several women, who have thereby stopped an attack almost before it began.

It's highly unlikely, but let's say that all of these physical self-defense methods fail for one reason or another. Or more probably you just can't use them. And your life is still in danger. What then?

In a word—anything. Or at least anything *action*-oriented. Perhaps you remember earlier in the book where I talked about what doesn't work in the assault situation. I said that struggling, hitting, kicking, using purse weapons, etc., were worthless except in one special situation. Well, this is the situation: when you are in immediate danger of your life or severe bodily harm and *all else has failed* . . . and you want to live.

You can stop worrying about whether or not you're antagonizing your assaulter now. It doesn't matter anymore. Your survival must come first. So if you're desperate, if for one reason or another you haven't been able to use any of the sure-fire self-defense methods I've described, hit, punch, kick, gouge, flail away—you may in this one situation even include screaming or yelling, though you should put your emphasis on fighting him, on action-oriented behavior—do anything except stand there and let your assaulter carve you up or shoot you or whatever.

If you and I have been on the same wavelength for the last couple of chapters, you know that there are lots of better ways to defend yourself against an assaulter than using some common object you might be carrying—an umbrella, a hardcover book, a purse or something similar

—as a weapon. Still, if you are in immediate danger of your life or severe bodily harm (and *only then*, I hope), and if you are unable or unwilling to use any of the other techniques I've described, you may be tempted to use such objects as weapons. For that reason, I consider it important to tell you the right and wrong ways to use them, however much I may disapprove.

The main rule: you should rarely, if ever, *swing* a weapon at your attacker. You'll be inclined to do just that, I'm afraid, with an umbrella or a pocketbook. If you swing a weapon it can be easily intercepted, taken from you and used against you. Swinging also increases the distance between you and your target, because you have to back swing, move away from your mark, to get leverage and momentum. Your back swing initiates movement prior to actual contact and uses up precious seconds, allowing your assailant time to adjust and react. This is called "telegraphing," letting him know what's coming. And as if these reasons weren't enough, even if you hit your assaulter a solid blow on the noggin, one hit probably won't put him out. And how many chances do you think he'll give you?

What you should do, if you *must* use a common object as a weapon, is to grasp it firmly with both hands, with the sharpest point—the corner of the book, the end of the umbrella, etc.—facing your assailant, them ram the point into his upper-lip area with all your might. The upper lip is densely populated with nerve endings, so if your blow is hard enough it will cause a great deal of pain. Will this be enough to temporarily incapacitate the assaulter so that you can get away? Honestly, I don't know. It depends on your strength, his pain threshold, how pointed the object you've chosen is, how good your aim is, how hard you thrust it, whether he had time to move his head back— taking some of the force from your blow—and several other factors. You see now why I'm not enthusiastic about using common objects as weapons. Still, when you are in immediate danger of your life and nothing else has worked, you should do *anything* that might incapacitate your attacker.

A word of caution is in order here, though. Since the assault situation breeds hysteria, and no one is immune from that, your situation will probably look much worse than it is. Remember: *few women are seriously injured during a rape. Even fewer are murdered.* The methods we've just discussed are intended only to prepare you for a really extraordinary circumstance—when all else has failed and you find yourself in immediate danger of your life or severe bodily harm. Tuck these ideas—especially the best ones, the eye push and the testicle squeeze—away in some corner of your mind and let them be. They'll be there if and when you need them.

Anything you do in immediate defense of your life or to prevent severe bodily harm is fair and even legal, but no one can tell you that you should fight violence with violence. What you are willing to do depends upon your frame of reference, your upbringing, your values, your view of yourself and the world. You may prefer to submit to penetration rather than harm your assaulter. Submitting to penetration *is* within the limits of reacting safely. If it doesn't help you, it won't harm you or at least threaten your life provided you don't struggle. If this is your choice, that's what you should do—no matter what anybody else says. It has to be *your* decision. On the other hand, you may feel that any technique, no matter how drastic, is justified to avoid rape on injury. If so, do what you feel you should. And never feel guilty about whatever method you choose to minimize the total physical or mental harm to yourself. Only *you* know what you're perceiving in such situation, and only *you* know what is valid for you to do.

7

Making a Date
for Rape

It's only an educated guess, but from all the evidence I've been able to collect over the years, I believe that approximately 35 percent of rapes are committed by a woman's own date, boyfriend or even fiancé.

Hardly any of these rapes are reported to the authorities, and I know about them only because of the women who have approached me after a lecture to tell me what happened to them, or through women who have reported such episodes to NOPRA (National Organization for the Prevention of Rape and Assault) in New York.

It is not that 35 percent of the time a woman goes out on a date she's going to be raped or that 35 percent of the women who date will be raped by their dates. What happens is that of the women who *are* raped, 35 percent of them are raped by their dates in what started out as a social situation.

This is an odd statistic and the longer you think about it, the stranger it seems. Can women be so unlucky or so foolish about whom they choose to go out with? Can men be so oblivious to what the women really want? Are some women inclined to accept dates from men who have a tendency to rape? Or is it possible that men in general find rape often irresistible when they're alone with a woman they consider attractive?

I don't think women find rapists unusually attractive, or, for that matter, particularly repulsive physically. All sorts of men rape. And I don't think that all or even any large minority of men will rape merely because they have the opportunity. The evidence against this hypothesis is just too strong.

Yet a disproportionate number of rapes occur on dates. Why? The answer, I think, lies in the very nature of dating, which is a complex social interaction between a man and a woman governed by a combination of their personalities (their psychologies and physiologies), the environment and the prevailing morality. It has strong sexual overtones, and nothing with strong sexual overtones is ever simple.

You might say that dating is one of the main battlegrounds of the war between the sexes. In this war, each side apparently has the same objectives: companionship, sex, finding a more permanent partner, gaining peer-group approval, increasing personal self-esteem.

But the sides differ on the importance of each objective. They also differ on how to achieve them, whether by subterfuge, persuasion, bribery, or, on occasion, even force. Sometimes, with luck, two partners in the dating situation get past the social games, to genuine openness and honesty. When this happens there can be a meeting of the minds. A relationship can form. Real emotion arrives on the scene. Eventually, with more luck, love grows.

Most of the time, though, at least in the beginning, a man and a woman on a date tend to play out the masculine and feminine roles society currently favors. So they start out with a preconceived notion of what the date should be, how they should act, and how their date should act.

This is especially true in the area of sex. Each partner has different *expectations* about how the evening will turn out sexually. The difference between them may amount to nothing more than whether the evening will be capped with two good-night kisses or one. Or it may be a more significant difference of opinion as to what the sexual activities will include. You may have different *limitations and potentials* about this particular evening, this particular partner. In general, though, a man has been taught that whatever the woman allows is fine, and many men will test until they are sure their date has reached her absolute limit.

Lastly, you have different responsibilities. That means you have to watch out for yourself on a date. And he has to watch out for himself. That much you'd both do, without thinking about it. But since dating is an interaction and since there's more to human relationships than self-interest, there's another angle to this responsibility. Each of you have to watch out for the other, at least to some degree. Your behavior will have an effect on him and you should take responsibility for it. The same goes for him.

Given the role of dating in our society and given your personal differences, you and your date may have conflicts even before you meet. They may be trivial, not even worth an argument, well within your ability to compromise. Or they may be serious enough to ruin your evening, serious enough, *if mishandled*, to result in rape.

Today's morality has served only to emphasize the conflicts. The double standard, out-of-date as it is, and perhaps always was, still lives. By this strange theory, sex outside of or before marriage is fine for men but not for women. But unless homosexuality becomes the rule, the only place a single man can get the sex the double standard allows him is with a woman, who isn't allowed to give it to him. The result: conflict.

On the other hand, an atmosphere of sexual permissiveness, real or not, tends to raise a man's expectations. It also confuses a woman's view of what her own limitations should be. The result: more conflict.

Conflict between two people on a date doesn't make rape certain. Most of the time, when there's a disagreement on sexual matters, the man keeps trying and the woman keeps saying no until they part. Or perhaps someone's mind gets changed. So the conflict is either settled or shelved. Sometimes, the partners agree to disagree, though both of them may have doubts about their decision. Sometimes one or both partners resolve not to see the other again.

It takes more than preexisting conflicts to cause rape on a date, of course. Everyone who dates has preexisting conflicts and not every date ends in rape. But these conflicts, these differences between the partners, are the root cause for the rapes that do occur on dates. It's when the conflicts aren't recognized by one party or both, when something happens to heat them up rather than cool them down, when they're mishandled by either partner or both, or when the attempt to resolve them comes too late that the stage is set for rape.

About six months ago a young woman came up to me after a lecture and described how she'd been raped by her date.

Gayle, an attractive eighteen-year-old, had gone out on a second date with Mike, a good-looking fellow who was a starting half-back on the varsity football team. Their first date had been with another couple and had ended with a good-night kiss.

Gayle described what happened next. "A couple of days later, Mike called and asked me out for that weekend. He also asked me if I was still dating Jim, a friend of his. I guess he'd seen us walking around, holding hands, or maybe Jim's arm was around me. We were always very affectionate. I told him the truth—I'd broken up with Jim more than a week ago.

"Anyhow, he suggested that we have a picnic dinner. He knew a beautiful spot in the park where we wouldn't be bothered by anyone, he said. Well, we were having a sort of Indian summer—it hadn't even started to get cold yet. And a picnic sounded like a good idea. I said yes."

I remember how Gayle looked when she said this—as if saying yes was her first mistake. Actually, she made her first mistake before that, as we shall see.

"I was really excited about it, you know. I really liked him. And I was still hurting because of Jim. Jim had wanted me to prove I loved him—you know what I mean—and I couldn't do it.

"It was all wonderful, for a while," Gayle went on. "He got me laughing right away. He has a way of saying things funny.

"The spot he'd found in the park was just perfect, soft, grassy, lovely, private. It was really quite romantic. I spread out a tablecloth I'd brought along and we had dinner. He'd brought beer. I'm not much of a beer drinker, but he made fun of me when I turned it down. He said I shouldn't act like a little girl. So I had a can. Two, I think.

"After dinner we played with a Frisbee for a while as the sun went down. Pretty soon, I was pretty tired and out of breath. Mike went to his car, came back with an old army blanket. We spread it out on the grass and lay down. We could see the stars by then."

At this point, the young woman hesitated. I thought for a moment she wasn't going to tell me the rest of the story, though I could have guessed it. "Then you started necking?" I prompted.

"Well, yes," she said. "It was the natural thing to do."

"I couldn't agree more," I said.

"We did a lot of kissing, at first. Wasn't anything wrong with that," she said. "Kissing isn't that important, is it? And we hugged a lot."

Gayle then described how after forty-five minutes the kissing developed into something more than she was prepared for and how, before she could do anything about it, her date was on top of her, undressing her.

"I sort of pushed at him, but he was much bigger and stronger than I was."

"Did you say anything more to him?" I asked.

She told me that she'd asked him to get up, that she'd even suggested going to a movie. "He said, 'A movie? Now? You gotta be kidding.' Then he started unzipping his pants . . . I told him I didn't want to do anything more with him—now or *ever*."

"And then?"

"And then he raped me," she said.

"Did you try to stop him?"

She told me she'd said "Stop" again and again, but he ignored her, except for once when he said, "You got no complaint, babe, you led me on." She tried to struggle, she said, but he was nearly twice her weight and almost a foot taller.

"Did you say you'd tell the authorities?"

"Afterwards, when he was taking me back to the dorm. And he said, 'You go ahead and do that, babe. No one forced you to lie down with me on that blanket, you know."

By now, there were tears in the young woman's eyes and some of the other coeds who'd come up to talk to me after my lecture were looking at us strangely. I had more questions, but I held back.

"You know what my roommate said when I got back?"

"What?"

"She asked me if I had a good time."

"What did you tell her?"

"I told her it was nothing special. Then I shut up. I couldn't tell her or anyone else what had really happened."

I've described this particular case, but I could have chosen any one of dozens of others. What happened to Gayle has happened to thousands upon thousands of other young women—and it needn't have. And not just women in their teens but in their twenties, thirties, forties, fifties.

Gayle—and most of the other women who've had experiences like hers—got raped because she didn't recognize the conflicts that are part of the dating situation, because she unwittingly heated up the conflicts rather than cooling them down, and because she wasn't careful enough about her behavior in general. And most of all, because of the way our society has conditioned Mike to the dating experience, and because Mike treated Gayle as an object instead of a human being.

Before she'd ever even talked with Mike, Gayle started off wrong, by her behavior with her ex-boyfriend. They'd apparently walked with his arm around her, and very likely they'd hugged and kissed without much caring who was watching.

There's nothing at all wrong with hugging and kissing. It would be a hell of a world without them. In fact, I'm not prepared to make a moral judgment about any sort of behavior that harms no one. But I am willing to make a practical judgment. When Gayle and Jim were openly affectionate around campus, other men—or, at least, Mike—got ideas about Gayle. Mike apparently thought, "Well, if they hold hands and kiss in public, just imagine what they do in private. Why can't I get some of that?" What she had done, in effect, was to tease him—unwittingly, no doubt, and indirectly. The effect: his *expectations* of the amount of sex he'd have with her when they dated were raised far above the normal level.

Gayle might have been more discreet with Jim, if she'd thought about it, and if she'd decided that was what she wanted to do. But in some circumstances, women indirectly tease men without actually doing anything at all. A fellow may take out a young woman he's heard "goes all the way." The rumor may be totally untrue, but that doesn't matter—his sexual expectations of her when the two of them date will still be higher than they would be if he'd heard no rumors. And his demands will probably mirror his expectations.

Women indirectly tease men whenever they do anything in public view that might lead others to believe they've had or they're having sex with someone. I'm talking mostly about public displays of affection, but there are other things that could give this impression.

Nowadays, a lot of young men and women set up house-keeping without the benefit of matrimony, which is surely their own business. But there may be some men around who think otherwise. These men figure that any woman who's willing to live with, and obviously sleep with, a man without marrying him is an easy mark. The truth is that a living-together relationship may be as stable as a marriage and based on the same emotions. The woman may be totally monogamous. But to a man whose brain has been saturated, almost from birth, with the double standard, she'll look promiscuous.

Later, the couple living together may break up. Marriages break up too (and divorced women face exactly the problem I'm talking about). Then the vultures move in, sure the woman is a pushover, maybe even convinced that in offering to have sex with her, they're doing *her* a favor, satisfying an acquired taste. Some men may not wait for the couple to break up. They feel that since she's "putting out" for one guy, there's no reason she shouldn't for two. When the couple who are living together are also sharing a house with some other couples or singles, the odds of such things happening increase dramatically. This also happens readily with married couples who party together.

Again, as we discussed in earlier chapters, this is not the woman's fault, but the fact remains that indirect, unconscious teasing can have unforeseen consequences that every woman should be aware of.

Gayle's second error, I think, was in accepting the kind of date she did. She knew, in advance, that she and Mike were going to spend at least the early part of the evening in a very private spot in the park. And she made no objection. Mike turned out to be the kind of Neanderthal who always reads sexual implications into a woman's friendly behavior. The same thing can happen when a woman consents to sitting in a parked car with a man or when she leaves a singles bar with him, where the game is defined that way in advance.

Again, I'm not saying a woman should never go to a private spot with her date. I think there'd be something wrong with her if she didn't want to, with the right guy at the right time. But Gayle had no way of knowing if Mike was the right guy. She hardly knew him.

There are other dangerous environments besides parks, parking lots, beaches, your apartment or his where you and your date are totally alone. Certain kinds of parties, for example, held in a private house or apartment.

Last year, when I gave what was my second lecture at a large university in Alabama, a woman who was hearing me for the second time told me what had happened to her when she went to a fraternity party on a first date. When she and her date arrived, they found what you often find in fraternity house or apartment parties: mass chaos. The records were blaring, the liquor was flowing, the couples were disappearing from the main room for fifteen or twenty minutes, then reappearing.

"I started dancing with my date," she said, "and before I knew it, we had danced right into a bedroom. At first I thought it was pretty funny. He started to get a little fresh, but it wasn't anything I couldn't handle.

"Then another guy came in. They both started wrestling with me, sort of. I still didn't think anything of it. We were all having fun. Then I realized that the pair of them were taking off my clothes. It slowly occurred to me that they had more in mind than fun and games.

"Well, I started struggling. I know that you said in your lecture that struggling was bad, but I couldn't think straight at first. The struggling didn't do me any good. Each one of them had grabbed hold of an arm and a leg and they were holding me down on the bed with no trouble at all. I realized I'd better think of something or I was going to be raped then and there.

"So I said, 'Okay, let's do it. But let's do it one at a time.' That seemed to make sense to them. One fellow headed for the door. Then I turned to the other one. 'Listen,' I said, 'would you mind turning around while I get undressed? I don't like being watched while I take my clothes off.' He snickered, shrugged and turned around.

"Then I ran out of the bedroom. I also ran out of the fraternity house into the street. In five minutes, I was back in my dorm. I wasn't raped, I wasn't beaten, and I'd learned a good lesson. The next time I go to a party like that, I'll make sure I really know the fellow I'm with."

I think this woman did very well, even though she made the mistake of struggling at the start. You should expect to make mistakes at first. It's what you do *immediately* afterward that counts. In other words, the mistake can't last *too* long. I also think she drew the right lesson from the experience.

To get back to Gayle, her next mistake was drinking beer when she really didn't want to and wasn't used to it. Now, I don't know if the beer played much of a part in her rape, but it might have. Ogden Nash's doggerel "Candy is dandy but liquor is quicker," has made a joke of it, but some Neanderthals still try to get women drunk so that they can do what they want. Many men, before a date, tell the woman, "Don't eat or drink anything, we're going to have refreshments." What he doesn't tell you is that *you're* going to be the refreshments.

Liquor is not sexually stimulating. It tends to slow the body functions, as a matter of fact. But it does break down your inhibitions as does marijuana. Marijuana does this so well that frequent users swear it's an aphrodisiac, that it actually makes you want to have sex. Research shows otherwise. The sexual feelings are there all the time. The marijuana just lowers your inhibitions, so you can perceive the sexual feelings you blocked or didn't notice, so you're less able to exercise your *responsibility* to yourself or your partner.

I'm not going to advise you to drink or not to drink, to smoke or not to smoke. But you should do whatever you do while being aware of the possible consequences.

Let me get back to the case of Gayle and Mike. The next mistake she made was to assume that "kissing isn't that important, is it?" Kissing is a very potent sexual activity all by itself. The upper lip is one of the most sensuous areas of the body. Either a man or a woman could be as enticed sexually by passionate kissing as by fondling direct sexual areas of the body.

Gayle got into trouble with Mike not only because she didn't realize how powerful a stimulant kissing is, but also because she didn't know that men become sexually aroused at probably a faster rate than women—at least overtly. This is mainly due to the different societal conditioning of men and women, notably the fact that men are led to believe that they are to be the aggressor. Women are to be passive; they're supposed to wait. The efficacy of this conditioning is evident in the respective peer-group pressure men receive from men—and from women. Therefore, whether or not men are actually (psychophysiologically) sexually enticed faster or not, in the living experience this assumption becomes fact. Every stimulus they receive forces this response—and the opposite for women. But this, I believe, is slowly beginning to change.

Still, women cannot always use their own reactions as a guide to when to put a stop to things. From Mike's standpoint, Gayle was leading him on, teasing him. She may not have meant to. She probably didn't. But that's what he perceived. That's what most men would have perceived in a similar situation. By allowing as much as she did, by putting up no convincing stop signals, Gayle led Mike to what, for him, was the point of no return.

While this often happens when the woman doesn't know the man she's going out with very well, it can also happen when they're apparently very close. Four years ago a young woman came up to me after a lecture and told me of a horrible experience she'd been having. She was engaged and the wedding was set to take place in a few weeks. She'd known her fiancé more than a year. She didn't believe in sexual intercourse before marriage, though she didn't object to heavy petting. During the last month, her fiancé had raped her repeatedly, the most recent time being the night before the lecture.

"It all started about a month ago," she told me. "Bill just wasn't himself. We went out and parked and he was very rough with me. I went back home, thought about it and started to wonder if he was the right guy for me."

The next time they saw each other, she told me, she wasn't willing to go as far with him sexually as she had been before. By the time the evening was over he'd ripped off her clothing and raped her.

"When I got back to the dorm, I called him and said I wanted to break the engagement," she said. "He turned me down flat. He said it was all my own fault—all that teasing, all that promising and no follow-through. He said he'd waited long enough."

The woman told her fiancé that she was going to tell her father what happened and her fiancé responded by saying he'd "beat her father to a pulp." And he was big enough to do it, she told me. So she went out with him again—and got raped again. She tried once more to break up with him, failed, went out with him once more and got raped once more.

"Why don't you go to the authorities?" I asked.

"Well," she told me in tears, "the wedding invitations have already been sent out. My parents would be mortified."

I said to her, "You're going to be living with that bastard for forty years just because you don't want your parents to be embarassed?"

With her permission, I got in touch with the school's dean of women. Bill was called in and ended up transferring to a school some two hundred miles away.

No matter how unmercifully he thought he'd been teased, Bill had no right to rape his girlfriend. Some men seem to believe that when a woman teases, or they think she does, which is usually the case, all the normal social rules no longer apply, that they then have the right to take whatever they want. In our society, that's called being emotionally disturbed. And "taking whatever you want" is known as rape.

During a lecture in Colorado last year, one young man asked me, "What do you think of a woman who goes almost all the way, and then chickens out?"

My answer literally put him in shock. I said, "This is America. And that, to me, means freedom of choice to do anything—as long as you don't hurt someone else. It has to be for *everybody*. That's what freedom's all about. Therefore, if making love is on a point scale from zero to ten, and a woman goes to point nine and wants to stop, she has the *right* to choose not to go any further."

Teasing, whether real or imagined, doesn't relieve a man of the responsibility for his actions but the woman must also bear responsibility for hers. In my opinion, neither the woman who had been raped by her fiancé nor Gayle, who went to an isolated park with a man she hardly knew, took any responsibility for the effect the sexual contact had on their partners. (Neither did either of the men.)

I'm not saying now that a woman must let a man make love to her if his desire for her is urgent. She's *never* obligated to do that. But it seems to me that she is obligated to communicate her limits, both for her sake and for her date's.

Don't think that you can keep a man at bay, sexually speaking, by allowing liberties. Many women do this, hoping that it will prevent demands they're not willing to meet. If you don't want to have intercourse this is exactly the wrong way to prevent such demands. If you allow a man to take sexual liberties he'll only be further aroused—and that much more likely to want to go all the way.

Every time a man asks a woman for a date, a kiss, a hug or even sexual intercourse (and he doesn't have to do it in words), he's putting his ego on the line. He's risking rejection—and the feeling that he's not attractive, not lovable, that he doesn't measure up somehow. In effect, he's crawled out on a limb and given the woman the saw.

And every time she uses that power to reject him in a manner he cannot accept, she hurts him. For example, Gayle said, "I told him I didn't want to do anything more with him—now or *ever*." She damaged his image of himself. Whatever his level of self-confidence, a man will still be a little less confident the next time he asks a woman for— well, just about anything. And if he doesn't see himself as such a hot shot to begin with, her rejection may be devastating.

That doesn't mean every rejected man will rape. Practically every man in the world has been rejected time and time again and done nothing more about it than sneak away to lick his wounds.

For rejection to trigger rape, there have to be the other factors we've discussed: preexisting conflicts, teasing or the perception of teasing, sexual arousal on his part, peer-group pressures, drinking, drugs, and an environment in which anything can happen.

Even if *all* of these factors are present, and to a high degree, your rejection of your date won't necessarily trigger rape unless for some reason his self-image is already in danger. This can happen if he's been having trouble at school or at the office, or with other women, or with his friends. It can happen if he hasn't been able to get rid of a fresh crop of acne, or if he thinks he's starting to lose his hair. It can happen if someone tells him his clothing is out of style or if he loses his job or doesn't get a raise. It can happen because of significant events or trivial ones that are significant to him. The important thing is not what has happened, but how he perceives it—and how he perceives himself as a result of it.

If all the circumstantial factors are present, and if your date's self-image is already weak, he may be impelled to rape you if you reject him in a manner he cannot accept. Your rejection may be the last straw. It may send him into a rage and lead him to do things he'd usually never even consider but now feels are perfectly justified. But rape is *never* justified.

And there's *no way* you can be sure if all the factors are present. You'll know about the circumstantial ones, *if* you think about them, but you can't know what's going on inside his head. What he's been saying to you probably won't provide any clues, because on a date both of you are trying to look your best in the eyes of the other. He's trying to look strong, masculine, intelligent and completely to-gether—no matter how he feels. Don't fool yourself into thinking you know the man just because you've gone out with him a few times.

In one case I know of, a woman in Oklahoma was raped and murdered because she rejected her date in a manner he couldn't accept. She was the kind of person who had a great deal of sympathy and concern for someone who was down and out. She evidently started seeing a man who fit that description and got somewhat involved with him, per-haps out of pity. They made love a couple of times. One night, according to the story he later told the police, he was impotent—and she laughed at him. Afterward, the man said, he realized that it had just struck her funny, that she wasn't putting him down. At the time, though, he was in-furiated enough to choke her to death.

The best thing you can do to avoid being raped is to break up the long chain of circumstances and events that can lead to rape during a date, especially if you don't know your partner well.

First, if you don't know your date well, exercise some control over your environment (a more important consid-eration than the clothing you're wearing, contrary to popu-lar consensus). Don't let him take you to a secluded place or to a wild party. Double-date. Go to movies, plays, con-certs, lectures, restaurants—anywhere there are people. After you get to know the man reasonably well and after he gets to know you, you can relax the rules, as you choose.

Second, don't drink, especially on an empty stomach. Don't use drugs either. Besides being illegal, they can lower his inhibitions or yours and involve you in sexual intercourse when you don't want to be having sexual intercourse. I know too many cases of women on drugs being raped—especially gang-raped.

Third, don't go out with just anybody. Even if you meet what seems to be the nicest fellow you've come across yet, get some feedback on him through others before you go out with him, if you can. Use your common sense. *Be aware*. Always know what's happening. Know your own expectations, limitations, potentials and responsibilities and those of your partner.

Communicate with your date. Presumably, one of the reasons you're going out together is that you want to get to know each other better.

Remember Bill, who raped his fiancée? When he was unusually rough with her, she should have asked him about it. He might have had a satisfactory explanation. She should have expressed her discomfort and he might have responded lovingly. For one reason or another, that heart-to-heart talk never took place, even though they were engaged. They didn't have enough trust in each other to share their thoughts and feelings—even the unpleasant ones, even the ones involving sex. At least partly because they didn't communicate, I think, their relationship ended in rape.

This lack of communication also exists in most marriages. When husbands and wives don't talk about their sexual expectations and desires, the same kinds of brutality result.

Under American law, it is impossible for a wife to sue her husband for rape. And in almost every part of the world the marriage contract is considered to dictate that it is the woman's duty to do her husband's bidding, whatever her own inclination. But it is *wrong* that the marriage contract should cause the woman to lose her rights as a human being.

The only way your date or boyfriend or lover will ever know your limits is if you communicate them. If you allow him to take you back to his apartment, you're saying one thing about your limits. If you're willing to go to Nantucket with him for a weekend, you're saying another thing about your limits. And if you allow him to take you to the movies, or a band concert or a football game, you're saying something else entirely.

Still, there's no substitute for talk. You may be unwilling to talk about sex with your date, your boyfriend, your fiancé or even your husband (and he might not be so willing either). Maybe it's because you feel embarrassed, inadequate or unprepared. Maybe you think you'd rather not commit yourself. Maybe you think talking about it amounts to teasing, all by itself. Maybe you think sex should be spontaneous, not premeditated, or that sexual activity isn't quite as sinful if it isn't discussed in advance.

Whatever your reason, if you don't find some way to communicate your limits you'll probably find yourself fending your companion off eventually. By that time, his needs will be more important to him than establishing communication with you.

The next piece of advice will be familiar to you: *treat him as a human being.* There's one crucial moment on a date where this may make the difference between having a good time and getting raped. It's the moment when you've reached your outside limit, where you have to say no. How can you do it without hurting him—perhaps so badly he'll want to hurt you back? The reason you should show concern for his feelings—even though it's he who's doing wrong—is to defuse the violence he feels toward women. You are doing this to prevent rape.

The best way to behave in this situation is to act toward him the way you'd like someone to act toward you if you were the one being rejected. You have to give evidence that you respect the trust that has been offered to you and that you have some concern for the man's feelings.

If necessary, take the fault on yourself. Tell him it's not him, it's you—that you've been taught certain ways to behave and that if you ever came to the conclusion you were wrong he'd be someone you'd like to be wrong with. Tell him you're not ready, though you may be at some time later.

If he says that it's the only way he'll believe you love him, tell him that the only way you'll believe he loves you is if he respects your moral code and that you could never do anything like that with someone you weren't sure loved you.

Don't make him feel undesirable, foolish, unworthy of wonderful and beautiful you, or unattractive, uncouth, uncool, unskilled or anything else un. See the good in him and tell him about it.

It's true that a man can be hurt if he's rejected. But that doesn't mean he has to succeed every time. You don't have to give in simply because you're afraid of hurting him. You can and should say no, if that's what you want to do. But do it in a way that preserves his self-image. Do it gently. Treat him the way you'd like to be treated. Treat him as a person.

You've probably noticed that this is much the same kind of behavior I advocated when dealing with a rapist. I'm not recommending it now because I think your date or boyfriend is a rapist but because I think that's the way you should behave with everyone, no matter what the situation, whether or not there's any threat to you. This is the way to get along best in the world. It's the way to make friends, to love and be loved, to relate closely to your fellow human beings. In that sense, what I'm recommending is more than a way to avoid rape. It's a way to establish good human relations with whomever you meet.

In spite of all the precautions you take, in spite of all the care you exercise when rejecting the demands of the man you're with, matters may reach a point beyond care and courtesy. His needs and expectations, your availability and your past relationship may make it impossible for him to stop—without help.

Now what? You don't want to put out his eyes or smash his testicles. You may even want to go out with him again. Is there any way you can turn him off without shattering every chance for a happy relationship?

A woman who'd heard my lecture at a university in North Carolina provided me with the following technique and I thank her for it. One night her fiancé became extremely demanding. There'd been a good deal of petting in their relationship but they'd never had intercourse.

Though his intentions were very clear, she couldn't think of her fiancé as a rapist. She loved him. She was planning to marry him within the next sixty days. She thought he loved her. Yet she did not believe in premarital intercourse.

She kept telling him to stop, but he kept kissing and caressing her and disrobing her. Finally, as he leaned up to kiss her, she turned away from him toward the window, stuck her finger far down her throat, turned back and threw up all over him.

His lust turned to sympathy. Inquiring solicitously about her health, he drove her back to her room and that was the end of that. She had turned him off in an instant.

The trick is easy to perform. Just stick a finger or two as far down your throat as you can. Nature will then take over.

To my mind, vomiting is the perfect defense against rape during a date. I can't imagine the man who could keep his mind on sex under such circumstances.

But won't he realize you've vomited on purpose? Probably not. Throwing up is the last thing he'll think you'd do. And if you've turned away from him slightly, he won't see you stick your fingers down your throat. Even if he sees you, he won't be in the mood for sex anymore.

I wouldn't use vomiting in the assault situation, where you've been attacked by what we call the "professional" rapist (in contrast to your date, who's probably never raped in his life). An assaulter may get upset if he understands you've thrown up on purpose and he may take his anger out on you. Your date is unlikely to be as emotionally disturbed as an unknown rapist.

If none of these techniques work, then you've gotten yourself into something other than a dating situation. You should treat the man no differently from the way you'd treat any other assaulter.

If these tactics fail, do what you think you must. Of course, if he's your boyfriend or your fiancé, and you love him, you may want to submit. But you don't have to. You have the weapons to use against him, if you wish to use them. If your fiancé or boyfriend or husband is going to rape you, you ought to take a good look at the relationship anyhow.

Despite the fact that rape can and does occur on dates, it would be a tragedy if that prevented a woman from dating. You ought to know the dangers of dating, but you also ought to know how to cope with them so that you won't be afraid and can enjoy the interaction of dating without being taken advantage of.

8

Friends, Romans and Kissin' Cousins

Approximately 35 percent of all rapes are committed by a man the victim has known in one way or another, briefly or for years. This is about the same percentage as rapes committed by the victim's date and in addition to that figure.

Included here are past boyfriends, ex-husbands, friends of the family, passing acquaintances, classmates, your roommate's boyfriend or brother or father, your brother's buddy, your neighbor, your best friend's husband, your husband's best friend, the clerk in the store you occasionally patronize, the mailman, milkman, gardener, handyman or delivery man, traveling salesman, your teacher, your student, your boss, your subordinate, a co-worker or a relative.

Of course, it doesn't mean a man's a rapist just because he falls into one of these categories and seems interested in you. The odds are ten thousand to one that he isn't.

On the other hand, whatever relationship a man and woman have, there is also at least the possibility that there can be a sexual relationship, though the thought may never enter either his mind or yours.

Very probably, if you get into a rape situation with someone you know, you're dealing with what we might call an "amateur" rapist, someone whose motives are more likely to resemble those of your date or boyfriend who comes on too strong, rather than of the man who has experienced a set of circumstances during his life that has left him with the urge to rape—although there is some correlation between the two.

Chances are, if you get into a rape situation with an acquaintance or a relative, it's because of his personal troubles (no doubt temporarily aggravated in some way), his image of you, his image of himself, the environment, whether or not he's been drinking, is on drugs or similar factors. As with dating, it's the combination that counts. Except in the case of rejected past boyfriends, the missing or hidden element will be that deep hostility toward women the "professional" rapist feels. For that reason, when you know your assaulter, only in the rarest instances need you fear bodily harm or injury.

That doesn't mean you don't have a problem. Rape by anyone is a problem. Dealing with someone you know who unexpectedly turns out to be a rapist can be harder than fending off a stranger, since some of the standard ways of handling a rapist aren't appropriate.

Obviously, you can't treat your Uncle Roger the same way you'd treat a guy who leaps out of the bushes and grabs you. If your livelihood depends on your job, you may be unwilling to squash one of your boss's testicles should he get persistent.

What can you do, then? Since the circumstances leading to the rape situation in these cases are much like those leading to rape during a date, and since you have a social relationship of some sort with the man, you can use the same tactics against him that you'd use against a date who demands sexual intercourse.

The key to protecting yourself against rape by someone you know is to be *aware*, at all times. You don't need to be suspicious of every male who comes near you, from your grandpa who is confined to a wheelchair to your ten-year-old cousin Billy who's always trying to look up your skirt. Act that way long enough and intensely enough and you won't be raped. You'll be institutionalized.

The awareness I'm talking about leaves your brain turned on at all times, your eyes open, helps you use your common sense, and realize you could be raped by *anybody*.

If you become aware that a friend, acquaintance or relative always tries to strike up a conversation about sex with you, or if he's looking at you with the sort of gaze you'd prefer he reserved for a topless dancer, or if he likes to touch and tickle as he did when you were, say, a seven-year-old, then it's time to turn the alertness up another notch.

The odds are still more than a thousand to one that he will ever do anything more than tease or maybe pinch. He's probably totally harmless, a fellow stuck in his own adolescence or maybe yearning to return to it. But some slight caution on your part may be in order.

Be aware of the sexual tension between you. If it stays on a low level you can let things be. If it is clearly increasing, take a couple of casual precautions to loosen it. Change the subject of conversation to something else you know interests him. Change the environment. If you're alone with him, go where there are people.

If you have any doubts about the man in question, or his mental state, or his sobriety, be aware of his behavior and, if possible, his perceptions of you and of himself. Be aware of your own behavior. Don't do anything you think he could perceive as teasing. Don't wear your flimsy night-gown in his presence just because he used to bounce you on his knee and you've known him for most of your life. Don't encourage conversation about your sexual experiences (or lack of them) or his. Put a firm halt to any inappropriate physical contact, but don't antagonize and don't humiliate.

If the situation continues to worsen, *communicate* your feelings to him as clearly as you can. Make sure he knows how you feel so that he cannot rationalize his behavior to himself by saying, "Well, she never really said I shouldn't or that she didn't *want* to."

Women are too often raped by past boyfriends or ex-husbands because they reject them in a way that damages their ego. Seeking to restore his ego, the man wants to put down his ex-girlfriend or ex-mate.

I know a case where a man and woman broke up, in part because he was unable to make love to her. She rejected him. Then, by chance, she started dating one of his friends who bragged about the sex he'd had with her.

I don't know exactly what went through the mind of the man who'd been rejected, but he called up the woman and asked for a date, "for old time's sake." She accepted, thinking there was no harm to it. They went out. He took her to a secluded spot, crudely approached her, was rejected again, beat her up, took a needle and thread and sewed her up.

The only way the woman could have prevented the ugly situation that developed was to find a way to build him up, rather than tear him down. As it was, the only options left open to her were physical self-defense techniques that she either didn't know or wasn't willing to use.

Care and caution *are* in order when you break up with a boyfriend, or a husband, for his sake and for yours. My records show that such men tend to be more violent than any other friends or acquaintances with whom you might find yourself involved in the assault situation, and even more violent and brutal than strangers. Your ex-boyfriend or ex-husband may not even have sex in mind. He may just want to beat you up. Understand, this is rare, but should it happen to you, there is a way out: transform his physical attack into a sexual assault. That won't be hard. It's just a matter of bringing up the subject, so to speak. Once the assault becomes sexual, handle it as you would an assault by a stranger.

The vendetta mentality that sometimes shows up in a past boyfriend or ex-husband can also show up in a man you've dated only a couple of times or in a man who's only flirted with you and perceived that you flirted back. There are cases like this where the man *perceives* he's a past boyfriend.

So the problem of how to reject without antagonizing also applies to the man who asks you out for the first time —assuming you don't want to be with him. Treat him the way you would your past boyfriend or a date who wants more from you sexually than you're willing to give. Never antagonize. Treat him as a person.

I wish it were an iron-clad rule that you're never in danger of bodily harm from an acquaintance who turns out to be a rapist. All I can say is that this is usually the case.

Among the exceptions, one of the most brutal cases I ever heard about was told me by Mary, a woman I met after a lecture. One evening there was a knock on Mary's door, and as she opened it she was greeted by Charlie, her roommate's boyfriend. Charlie asked where his girlfriend was and Mary responded by saying that her roommate had moved out, and added, "I would have thought that you knew that?"

Charlie asked if he could come in for a cup of coffee, and when she invited him in he immediately hit her, dragging her into the bedroom, slamming her onto the bed, tying her up, beating her. During all of this, Mary screamed and struggled and fought, terribly frightened. He put a revolver into her vagina and threatened to shoot it, at which Mary screamed even more.

Charlie took a knife out and drew it across various parts of her body, drawing blood. She tried to fight back the best she could with her hands and feet tied and screaming all the time. Her attacker then took clothing out of a bureau drawer, stuffed it into her mouth, choking her. Mary later told me that at this point she felt she was about to die and she looked up at him the only way that remained for her to communicate: imploringly, as if she would do anything he said. Somehow her assailant got the message. He took the things out of her mouth and untied her. Even through all of this hell, Mary understood that this was a man in trouble and realized that to survive she needed to help heal his wounds, not make them any worse. She invited him out into the kitchen for something to eat, treating him like any other guest in her apartment. At that point he told her he wanted to do several other grotesque things to her. She agreed, knowing the peril she was in, and he responded to her cooperativeness by leaving.

How could Mary have gotten out of this assault? She could have done exactly what she finally did do—turn the physical attack into a sexual encounter—only earlier. She could have prevented him from humiliating and degrading her by humbling herself, in his eyes. She could have gotten him close to her, then done away with him. It seems pretty clear to me that she could have justified whatever she did to him. She could have stopped the physical assault if she'd treated him as a human being. (I know he wasn't acting like one, but the tactic isn't intended as a reward for the assaulter. It's meant to protect the victim.) If she'd regained her emotional stability earlier and applied her imagination and good judgment, as she did near the end, she could have escaped the attack in other ways. She might have said, "I know where Sue is. She has an apartment nearby and she's alone. I'll take you there." Once out in the open, with other people around, she could have escaped. Though Mary wasn't actually raped, she went through a hell no one should have to endure.

One of the first assault cases I studied involved a woman who had heard a ten-minute introductory lecture of mine. Twelve weeks later, she was assaulted by a man who turned out to be her brother's best friend. He put a knife to her throat and forced her to drive out into the woods with him, threatening to kill her unless she submitted to penetration. She chose to submit, as the lesser of two evils.

Nothing further happened to her because she never revealed that she recognized him and she convinced him that she could not tell anyone about the rape because of her own embarrassment. She persuaded him to take her back to town. As I was studying this case and talking to her, Betty asked me, "I did as you said, didn't I? I went along all the way?" Betty was wrong. Going along all the way does *not* mean submitting to penetration. Going along all the way means to go along by taking an attitude that would gain his confidence, to make sure you represent no threat or risk to his security so that he relaxes his vigilance. It doesn't mean you must go along sexually. I know women are taught to believe that the most important thing about them is their body. That's wrong. The most important thing about a woman is her mind, her intelligence, plus her feelings, her emotions, her attitudes—what she is as a person, not as a body. This incident happened ten years ago in the South, and Betty truly believed that the most important thing she had to give a man was her body. Though she did save her own life, she might have gotten out of the assault even earlier by gaining his confidence proving that she was no threat to him, and persuading him to put down the knife.

A much more typical case was related to me only several months ago by a young woman named Barbara who had arranged to spend a weekend at a girlfriend's house. On Friday night the two young women spent a pleasant evening with the mother and father. The next morning the girlfriend and her mother went to the grocery store, leaving Barbara sleeping in the guest room and the father at home. About fifteen minutes after they left, the father knocked on the visitor's door.

"Barbara," he said, "are you up?" He opened the door and walked in before she could answer, though she was still in bed in her nightgown. He came over and sat down on the bed.

"You don't wear much makeup, do you?"

"No," Barbara said innocently. "I don't think I look good in it."

To her total astonishment, he leaned over, put his arms around her and kissed her. She hadn't realized anything was amiss until that moment. The father then told Barbara he wanted to make love to her. She was too shocked to reply.

Evidently, this was a planned assault. Though she started to struggle, she was embarrassed—it was her girlfriend's father. In no time at all he'd undressed and penetrated her.

After he reached his climax he got off the bed, told her he'd enjoyed that and hoped that she had also. Then without further conversation he walked out of the room.

"It was like a bad dream," Barbara told me. When her friend came back, she made some excuse and immediately left to go back to school. She'd never told another soul about it until she approached me after hearing my lecture.

There are a lot of things Barbara could have done to avoid being raped. She might have said, "How would you feel if your daughter was lying here—she could be, you know." Or, "How would you feel if this were happening to your daughter." Or, "Some of the kids at school think your daughter and I look alike—do you think so?"

If this sort of talk didn't bring him around, she could have used any of the tactics to avoid rape we've already talked about.

As it happened, she couldn't do any one of these things because she never regained her emotional stability. She probably hadn't regained it by the time she'd left or she would have said something, either to her friend or her friend's mother. She might not have been believed, but I would guess that mother and daughter would have been much more careful from then on when a female guest was in the house. That might have saved another woman from being raped.

I want to emphasize that though this case is typical of those in which a woman is raped by a friend, acquaintance or relative, it is exceptional in one way. Out of every ten thousand women who spend a weekend at a friend's house or baby-sit, probably fewer than one will be raped. Your chances of being confronted with this sort of situation are very, very small. In fact, as we have seen, your chances of being raped at all, under any circumstances at any time in your life, are minute.

Nonetheless, it will do you no harm to incorporate these ideas and tactics into your repertoire of knowledge, to be examined, then put into storage, for use when needed. Besides helping you in a particular circumstance, this information should lessen the shock and encourage emotional stability if you are attacked.

Another typical situation in which the rapist and the victim know each other involves a young baby-sitter and the father of the children she's taking care of. Usually, things go wrong here when the father drives the sitter home.

In one case, about halfway to the fourteen-year-old sitter's house, the father of the family suggested that they
have a hamburger. The girl refused, but the man pulled the
car off the road anyhow, into a secluded spot. Before long,
he was touching and fondling her.

"He wasn't brutal," the baby-sitter told me later, "just
extra-passionate. I tried to push him away, but he was
much stronger than I was. And he was very determined."

Before long, he began to strip her and take down his
pants. He was very near penetration by the time she thought
of something to do.

"You know, Mr. Jones," she told him, "in nine or ten
years this could be happening to your little girl."

The effect on the man was electric. He wilted like a dead
flower, apologized as he wept, and started pouring out his
troubles to her. They ended up talking for hours, reaching
a genuine understanding, and even became good friends.
The youngster continued to sit for the family with no further incident.

This young woman evoked her attacker's feelings of
parenthood. She elicited his empathy. She did not vindic-
tively put him down, by saying something like, "Mr. Jones,
you should know better than this!"

Treating the man as a human being was also exactly the
right thing to do, and it's an attitude that could and should
be adopted by any baby-sitter.

Relatives who do something or try something they
shouldn't represent a difficult and delicate problem. I'm not
talking now about kissing cousins who want to be kissing
—whatever that is, it isn't rape—but about uncles or cousins or nephews or even grandfathers who force their sexual
attentions on you.

Again, this kind of situation is the exception. There is no
need to take constant readings from every male relative.
But such things do happen, and, somewhere in the back of

your mind, you should be prepared. Relatives aren't immune to emotional disturbances nor to sexual desire, remember, or, to put it another way, every rapist is somebody's uncle, or brother, or father, or nephew, or son.

If a relative signals this kind of behavior, your first objective is, obviously, to avoid being raped; second, to make
sure your relative gets help. A relative isn't the same as a
casual acquaintance. You'll probably be coming into contact with him again and again over the years and unless he
solves his problem, you or one of your female relatives may
become engaged in a running battle.

Not only will you want to avoid rape and want to find
help for your relative, you'll also want to accomplish both
with the least physical and psychological harm to either of
you, or the rest of your family.

As with other people you know, the best approach to
turning off a relative who finds you a turn-on is to handle
him as you would a date.

The problem gets stickier if your relative's advances become so violent that they threaten your physical safety.
You have an obligation to yourself. But you also have an
obligation to your family. Who comes first? I feel you do.
But there's no way I can make this decision for you. You'll
have to depend on your own good judgment. You now
have the means to do away with him if you think you
must. But give it some thought . . .

If the odds are, say 10,000 to one that a relative will
ever try to rape you, I'd guess that they're a million to one
that such a rape situation could ever put you in immediate
defense of your life or severe bodily harm.

The trickiest problem you're likely to face if a relative
tries to assault you is how to get help for him.

I've had women come up to me and ask, "How do I go
to my father and tell him that my uncle . . . his brother . . ."
A good solution is to go to a member of your intimate

family who is not related by blood to your inappropriately passionate relative. If your molester is your father's brother, go to your mother. But don't do this if that person is exactly the one most likely to get violent or hysterical. Choose someone in whom you have the most confidence, the one most likely to be objective, who will offer help instead of moral judgments.

Your goal should be to have this objective relative or friend have a heart-to-heart talk with the relative who's made improper advances to you. The object: to get him to see a religious counselor or a guidance counselor, or, better yet, a psychologist or a psychiatrist.

I don't advocate calling the police in this situation. In most cases going to the police will threaten the entire family structure, turning relative against relative. He will be there, in the family, as long as he lives—there's no known way to unrelate someone.

9

The Gang

From what women tell me, they find nothing more terrifying than the thought of group rape, or, to use the vernacular, gang bang.

Group rape is a sexual assault by more than one man or by a mixed group of men and women. It can happen to you whether you're alone or not, and there are both differences and similarities between group rape and the sort of assault that involves only one assailant.

In both cases the object is to humiliate and degrade you via a sexual attack. Like the individual rapist, one or more members of the group most probably will be angry as hell at women in general—the anger is based on fears that are probably a result of real or imagined traumatic rejection by women they held in high esteem. Some gang rapes begin with two or more guys "messing around" with a woman they feel is willing. And maybe she is—for one. But in these cases, she is *forced* to perform for the crowd. In the group rape situation, the assaulters get their courage from collective action.

Surprisingly, perhaps, violence is rarer in group rape than it is with the lone assaulter. A lone assaulter usually feels insecure and may act on this feeling by being violent. Or the woman may struggle or scream or do something else antagonistic that forces him to be brutal. Gangs, on the other hand, have no reason to feel insecure. In numbers there is strength. Even if you struggle, you can be easily subdued by a gang. Even if you scream it's no problem to shut you up.

When violence does occur in group rape, the group is likely to be composed of both men and women, and the *women*, not the men, are usually violent to the victim. The main reason for this is probably jealousy. After all, just by choosing to rape a stranger, the gang has rejected its women. The women's revenge may be immediate and brutal. At the least, they'll be extremely unsympathetic.

In an incident that occurred in North Carolina in 1966 a couple had driven to a local lovers' lane and parked. Within a few minutes a mixed group of men and women surrounded their car. The young man leaped out of the car, ready to give his all for his girlfriend. He ended up tied to a tree. The gang then pulled the woman out of the car, dragged her over to within a few yards of the tree, held her down and started tearing her clothing off.

At first, the women in the gang were content to stand back and watch. But then the woman who was being raped made a mistake. She said something to the female gang members like, "Why don't you stop them? What kind of women are you? Are you enjoying this, too?"

The female gang members glared at her for a moment, then thoroughly antagonized, they attacked. They beat her breasts and face to a pulp; they didn't touch any other part of her body. And while they beat her they kept saying, "This ought to teach you," and "Nobody else will want you now!"

The men raped the woman, but they didn't otherwise harm her. Neither did they hurt her boyfriend. In fact, before they left they untied him.

The victim's mistake, of course, was to antagonize. But she might have been beaten up even if she'd kept her mouth shut. To repeat, the very fact that the men in the gang had wanted to rape her was an insult to the female gang members.

Group rape is governed by mob psychology, the same force that Hitler tamed and used against humanity. The French psychologist and sociologist Gustave Le Bon, wrote a book about the subject in 1895 called *Psychologie des foules*, which later appeared in English as *The Crowd: A Study of the Popular Mind*. What Le Bon discovered and Hitler put to use was that people react differently in crowds or groups than they do individually. They stop thinking for themselves and start responding to the prevalent emotion. I find this true when I'm lecturing: when I tell a joke to an audience of three thousand, I'm much more likely to get prolonged laughter than when I tell the same joke, under the same circumstances, to an audience of fifty.

As long as it stays together, the crowd, or the gang, is a society unto itself, with its own rules, its own mores, its own concerns. These may have little to do with the tenets of society in general. That's one reason there is such a thing as gang rape. Gang members can give each other "permission" to do something that society would never allow.

In addition, each gang member, and especially the leader, has something to prove to the others: his masculinity. What better way can an insecure, disturbed man demonstrate that than by raping some innocent woman—a cause of fear and torment throughout his past?

At the moment of the assault, anyhow, gang members often feel they bear little responsibility for what's happening—individually. The guilt and responsibility is divided four ways, or six, or however many there happens to be in the gang. Split up like that, it's no load at all, not in the excitement of the assault situation. Given this way of rationalizing behavior, the more members in the gang, the more likely they will rape.

The gang that rapes need not be a formal group, with a name and a clubhouse. It can merely be a group of men, one or more of whom has a low tolerance for stress in this area, who are thrown together for the moment, and while in the right frame of mind, come across a perfect opportunity for rape. That doesn't mean that every group of men carries with it the potential for group rape. Men who have a strong sense of their own values are resistant to mob psychology, as are men who have strong ties to society and support it. The men likely to participate in group rape— for that matter, the men most likely to join gangs in the first place—are weak, uncertain, confused, detached from society, unclear about their own values, insecure about their manhood or otherwise saddled with a poor self-image. They need to prove something and they need the support of others to help them.

Group rape is not uncommon. Of the rapes that are not committed by a woman's date or someone else she knows, they account for perhaps a third of the remainder. To put it another way, about 10 percent of all rapes are committed by groups, according to my own estimate and the information I have gathered over the years. Other authorities have come up with higher figures, ranging from 16 percent in a study done in Denmark to an astonishing 66 percent in a Finnish study. In the last case, I believe it's nothing more than a statistical oddity—that there were too few rapes in Finland during the year the study was made to come up with any solid conclusion about group rape. Studies done in the United States hold that groups account for anywhere from 18.5 percent of all rapes (Denver) to 43 percent of all rapes (Philadelphia). These statistics are not incompatible with mine, when you consider that all of these studies are dependent on police files, and as I pointed out earlier, these files cover a very small percentage of rapes, only the reported ones. A disproportionate number of reported rapes are group rapes, since, unfortunately, our male-dominated society finds rape by one man implausible—a barbaric attitude, I might add.

But the figures are totally meaningless to the woman who's been raped by a gang. There's no question that such an experience can be devastating. Many have been reported to me by the victims and their stories are horrifying.

One young woman was walking along the street just after dinner one night when a car loaded with a group of raucous farm workers pulled up beside her. It was nearly dark and no one else was nearby.

At first, the men just made remarks. They talked about her long blond hair and made obscene references to what she was like under the baggy sweatshirt and blue jeans she was wearing. Cindy started looking for some place to escape to, but there were no stores open in the area, nor any lighted houses. She was walking beside a park. It wasn't long before the men started urging her to get into the car with them. She refused, but the car stopped and one guy ran out, grabbed her and shoved her into the front seat. Then the car drove off.

There were four men in the car, Cindy told me, two in front, two in back. She found herself sitting between the two in the front seat. From the moment she realized what was happening to her, Cindy never lost her head. She kept thinking, looking for a way out.

"I went to your lecture last year," she told me, "and I remembered that you said to keep cool and retain your emotional stability."

At first, the men kidded around while she kept saying, "I have to get back to the dorm. It's getting late." She was trying desperately not to antagonize them while attempting to find a way out. They ignored what she said. As the men began to fondle her she tried to move out of reach, but as much as possible, without struggling. Though she was firm at first, but not aloof, she realized her dilemma and now did her best to make them think *she* thought they were just fooling around.

She almost playfully tried to stop the men from touching her. In reality, she was going along. Stalling. Thinking. Searching. She knew how dangerous the situation was, and its chance for explosion. Meanwhile the driver headed out of town into the country.

Cindy told me that she realized if they ever got her into the country, she'd be at their mercy. She figured that she had to find a way to stop the car. As they went around a curve, she grabbed for the wheel and tried to steer the car into a ditch. The driver pulled the wheel away from her and managed to keep the car on the road, though just barely.

That ended the fun and games. Cindy had committed her behavior. She had, in effect, struggled. The laughing and playful molesting stopped and she felt her clothes being ripped off.

Soon, the car stopped. The men pulled her out and carried her into a field. Then they took turns raping her. They forced her into several other sex acts. Terrified, she did her best not to struggle. She had good reason: one of the men in the car had displayed something shiny and had threatened her; she was sure he had a knife.

Her main goal now was to survive the assault. She did her best to appease the men who were raping her, to keep from getting hurt and to gain their confidence. But when they were finished with her, the first thing they did was to start arguing about whether or not to kill her.

"You don't have to do that," she told them. "I wouldn't have chosen to do this with all of you at once, but I'm not angry with you. There's no harm done, really. And I'm not going to run and tattle on you. What good would that do?"

Evidently, she was convincing. She even persuaded them to take her back into town, so she wouldn't have a ten- or fifteen-mile walk back.

The moment Cindy got back to town, she reported the rape to the police. They picked up the men on the basis of her description. She identified them. As it happened, they'd taken her across a county line, so they were charged with state kidnapping.

All things considered, I think Cindy did reasonably well. She came out of the assault unharmed—physically *and* mentally intact—though I know some mental scars must remain. But she could have done better. I think she could have avoided being raped.

The defense against group rape lies in the nature of the gang. Every gang, whether formal or informal, whether long established or together only for the moment, has a leader. He may be acknowledged openly by all, or he may be the tacit leader, the man who calls the shots, whether or not others in the gang are completely aware of it. This man is the key to your defense against group rape.

Should you find yourself assaulted by a gang, your first job is to spot the leader. It won't be hard and it won't take long. Most of the time, you'll know him because he'll be the one who gets to you first. You'll know who he is because either he'll be doing all the talking or everyone will be looking at him while they talk, seeking his approval.

Once you've spotted the leader, go to him. Tell him you

can respond better to him if the two of you are alone. "Let's you and me go off someplace—yours or mine, it doesn't matter."

Try your best to be what he wants. If he wants your blouse open, open it for him. Put his hand on your breast. Press against him. Tell him the two of you can really have fun together. But make him *believe* you.

Put your arm around him. Tell him he's good-looking, or strong, or well-dressed or make any positive comment you can. Build his ego. Do your best to become *his* woman. "You don't want to share me, do you? Let's go off alone. They can have me later, if that's what *you* want."

Don't belittle the rest of the gang, though. You may have the wrong man. Or the leader may feel you're belittling him indirectly. Don't say, "They're ugly, but you're handsome." Just say good things about him, and by your actions, show him that you mean them. Promise him whatever you think he wants.

The leader will be vulnerable to this approach. Like every other man, he wants others to see him as desirable or attractive. If you build his ego, you're satisfying that need. No matter how secure he might be as a leader of the gang, he wants his leadership reaffirmed. You're doing that by choosing him. Another factor is that he may not be overjoyed to put his manhood to a test by raping a woman in front of the rest of the gang. You're providing him with an "out" that he wouldn't dare take unless *you* offer it. By offering to be alone with him, you're offering him protection.

If you get the wrong man, the right man will let you know it in no time flat (before you've committed yourself too much), and all you have to do is transfer your allegiance. If there are two competing for the leadership, you'll know that quickly, too—as soon as you make your choice.

Go with the one who seems stronger, the one who commands respect from the majority. If you can't decide which one that is, choose either one. Your choice will end the competition. Don't play one against the other, though. You may end up in the middle. If, in either of these situations, you commit yourself to someone, then find out he's not the leader, try to convince the real leader that if each will take you off, separately, you'll be able to respond better. Yes, back to the same ploy. But the gang will recognize its truth and that will help you gain their confidence.

Once you have identified the leader and shown him you're interested in him, you're going to have to get him alone if you're going to avoid a group rape.

Be seductive. "Let's go anywhere you want—but let's go alone." "Let's take your car." Or, "I'd like to ride on your motorcycle." Tell him, "It's a cold night, wouldn't it be more comfortable in a cozy room somewhere—your place, or mine?" Say, "Let's have a beer first. It'll be more fun if we're a little looped, won't it?" Make him feel special.

If you do it right, and you do it in front of the gang, they'll end up pushing him to go along with you. He'll have trouble refusing you without losing face. I can't guarantee you it will work, but I do say that if you're insistent enough and persuasive enough and seductive enough, your chances of getting him alone are excellent.

And it is important that you really are alone. It is not enough to go off to the side of the road with him, twenty yards from the rest of the group. Go way off with him and leave them behind. The idea is that you're his, not theirs—at least not for a while.

Once you get him alone, you might be able to say to him that you were really afraid of those guys but that you knew he was strong enough or smart enough or commanded enough respect to protect you. Build his ego. Once you get him alone, you have a good chance of avoiding further advances altogether. He may need the backing of the group to take such a step as rape.

If he persists in his desires, treat the situation as you would any other assault. It's not group rape anymore. And the one real advantage in getting him alone—excluding the possible prevention of the actual assault as mentioned above—is that if you find yourself in immediate danger of your life or severe bodily harm, you can do away with your assailant. This would be all but impossible in a group.

What you've done here, of course, is something as old as the hills. You've followed the principle of *Divide and conquer.* This is the best way—and the only way—to deal with group rape when you are the lone victim. Just remember to follow the principle in the order you've heard it. First divide. Then conquer.

If for any reason you cannot separate the leader from his gang, your best bet is still to treat your situation as you would any other assault. Be especially careful not to antagonize. Treat each gang member not only as a human being but also as an individual. Go along—until you can safely react.

Even when the gang who assaults you consists of only two persons, you can still separate one from the other. You can identify the dominant partner and offer to go off with him. At the very least, you can probably arrange to take them on separately. And, when you're dealing with one at a time, there's plenty you can do, as you know.

I know of one case where a woman was grabbed and thrown into a car as she walked down the street. In this case, there were two men: the one who grabbed and the man behind the wheel. The man who'd grabbed the woman pushed her into the back seat, stripped himself and started to strip her. She didn't wait to be told what to do. She grasped his sex organ and started massaging him sensuously.

For a moment the guy was startled. Then a grin spread across his face. He encouraged her to continue. Just as he was about to reach a climax—and was therefore at his most defenseless and most distracted—she opened the door and jumped out.

The man was so startled, so close to orgasm—and so naked—that giving chase was out of the question. Besides, she had timed her escape for an area with people nearby when the driver had slowed down to watch and "get in on" the activity in the back seat. The man in front at the wheel never knew what happened until too late. This woman, on her own, brilliantly avoided being raped.

Things become more complex when you're not the lone victim of a group assault, when you're with a girlfriend, for example. It may still be possible to divide and conquer, and you should do it if you can. But your object should be not merely to avoid rape and injury, but also to get help for your friend, if possible.

Let's say you're with your girlfriend Beverly and you're attacked by three or four men. The moment it's clear that what's happening isn't simply an unpleasant conversation but an assault, Beverly starts beating the nearest assaulter with her purse and screaming. The man smiles uncertainly for a moment, then starts punching her with all of his might.

What do you do?

You don't rush to her aid. If you do, you'll be the next one to get punched out.

Your problem is that your assaulters won't differentiate between Beverly's behavior and yours. If she screams and struggles, it will be just the same as if you're also screaming and struggling. Even though you know better.

The way to deal with the problem is to separate yourself

from Beverly any way you can. Get away from her physically, if you can—twenty or thirty yards, if possible. If that
isn't possible, go to her and tell her to stop screaming or
stop struggling. Say, "Hey, relax. We're going to have a
good time. These are great-looking guys." Or whatever
comes naturally. Just take care not to shout through her
screams, so that your assaulters won't think you're screaming too. Slap her if you have to. Don't whisper, though.
That might give your assaulters the impression you're planning something. It won't hurt anything for them to hear
what you're telling her.

At the same time you're encouraging Beverly to go
along, you can tell your assaulters that Beverly is just upset,
that she's immature, that she doesn't understand the fun
she can have, that she's shy. "Let me talk to her and I'll
make it all right," you could say. Does this sound like
you're switching sides? If so, good. Believe me, for your
sake and Beverly's, you'll do better on their side than on
hers.

When I say, "Go along, be seductive," I also mean don't
be cheap about it. Don't act as if you'd do it for anybody.

Once you have your friend quiet and apparently submis-
sive, you have many options. The most logical is to tell the
men that you know another woman who'd like to join the
party. I know of a case where three women evidently escaped rape with just this ploy, by describing a "terrific-
looking woman" they would get. Instead of going for the
extra girl, they went for the police and they avoided rape
or whatever else had been in store for them.

I'm sorry to have to tell you this, but if you think being
with your husband, fiancé, boyfriend or date protects you
from group rape, you're wrong. He may make things worse
for you.

When group rape does occur, the dating situation is
often the setting. Usually, it happens when a woman is in a

parked car with her boyfriend. In the mind of the gangs, or some individual assaulters, this is the ideal time to humiliate a woman, as well as the ideal time to wreak havoc and vengeance on a male who *isn't* being rejected. This is done by making the man feel helpless while his date is viciously violated. Many of these assaults have elements of a vendetta—where the man is forced to watch. Caryl Chessman, who was executed in San Quentin for kidnapping, after spending almost twelve years on death row, used to prowl lovers' lanes for exactly this purpose. He'd drive up beside a car occupied by a couple who were necking, abduct the woman at gunpoint, then rape her.

If you and your date, boyfriend or fiancé are parking, there are some common-sense precautions you can take against assault, either by individuals or gangs. Make sure the car is parked in such a way that you can make a fast getaway if necessary. Leave the keys in the ignition. Make sure that the car is left facing out. Keep the doors locked and the windows rolled up—that will give you some valuable extra time in the event of attack. (Of course, if it's cold and you have to leave the motor running, leave at least two windows open just a crack. Too many people have died from carbon monoxide poisoning sitting in running parked cars.)

Don't park in lovers' lanes, especially if there are no other cars around. They're prime targets for gangs looking for trouble, or for assaulters. A better place to park is in town somewhere, in a row of parked cars, on a residential street or on a lightly traveled business street. If you park between street lights, you'll have plenty of privacy—after all, who walks along the street peering into car windows? This will not only protect you against gangs or assaulters, it will also protect you if your date gets out of hand. If anyone approaches, start the car immediately and get out of there.

Another way to protect yourself against group rape in the dating environment is to choose your date with some care. Pick a man who's mature enough to know that he doesn't have to defend your honor to a stranger, who's confident enough to know he doesn't have to challenge someone to show off his masculinity, who's smart enough not to get the two of you into trouble by initiating violence in your presence.

It wouldn't hurt, for your sake and his, if he had some knowledge of self-defense. Assaults on men are increasing. As a matter of fact, the rate of assaults on couples—men and women—is also increasing, and faster than the assaults on women alone. A man usually is not assaulted for sexual reasons and he therefore cannot convert a physical attack into a sexual one in order to save his life. A man further represents more of a physical threat to the assailant, and therefore has a far more difficult task in pretending "to go along" and thereby defusing the potential violence. So unless a man knows some physical self-defense techniques, he is less able to handle himself in such a situation than a woman is. Now, I don't mean you have to date a Tarzan. Though it's not easy, any man can learn to defend himself against the average one or two assailants in the street.

But note: the instructor is the most important single element in learning self-defense. He has to know how to adapt the course to the student, not vice versa. Everyone has personality traits, physical moves and attitudes that can be adapted to effective self-defense.

But even if a man knows self-defense techniques, he shouldn't use them unless the assaulter or gang initiates violence, or puts either or both of you in immediate danger of your life or severe bodily harm.

In general, when a man and woman are confronted with a group attack, flight is much better than fight. Chances are, if there is a fight the woman will be the door prize. If you both can't flee, then the man should try to occupy the gang while the woman runs to safety and calls the police. Most men will handle themselves better in a confrontation of this sort if they know their date is safe. And most gangs will be less eager to attack if there is no prize for the victor.

In the parking situation, if the man is dragged out of the car the woman should drive off immediately and get help. Or, if the circumstances are right, she can start up the car and use it as a weapon against the assaulters. I would even say that if the woman is dragged out of the car it might be to her advantage if the man leaves her, drives off and brings back help, fast. Unless he's the son of Kong, he alone won't be able to help her much in the group-rape situation. Literally every case I've studied shows that the average man in this situation makes matters worse, since he offers a challenge to the gang's security, and therefore increases the possibility of violence.

Much of this, I admit, is nothing more than common sense. Yet it's surprising how rare common sense is, especially in a high-anxiety situation like rape. In one case I have on file, a young couple was driving home from Sunday evening worship. They'd stopped along the road to have a "lovers' quarrel." Suddenly, they were surrounded by three teenage toughs, one of them brandishing a revolver.

"Get out of the car," the boy with the gun shouted. Since the car windows were rolled down, the doors unlocked, the keys in the man's pocket and the car facing in, the couple had no choice. They got out.

"Open the trunk," one of the gang members instructed the man. He did. "Now get in." He got into the trunk and the gang member slammed the lid.

Meanwhile the other members of the gang had taken the

woman into a field. They were taking turns raping her. They were also taking turns watching the trunk. One was always there.

"Hey in there," the gang members would shout to the fellow inside the trunk. "Are you all right?"

"Sure," said the man. "I'm fine."

The question was repeated several times. Evidently, the gang was worried that the man would suffocate. They were willing to risk punishment for rape but not murder. He kept reassuring each gang member that he was all right.

In this case, as it happened, the woman's date was quite a physical specimen, a top athlete. He was also a pretty good student. But he used neither his strength nor his IQ.

Eventually the gang left, without harming his date— except raping her a number of times. She was dazed, but she soon recovered enough composure to walk back to the car. The keys were in the trunk lock. She let her boyfriend out and he drove her home.

This man made two major mistakes. He parked on a lonely road and took no precautions, such as locking the car. Then, he kept telling the gang that he was all right. They were obviously worried about his condition. If he had kept quiet, or moaned, or choked and coughed, or said, gasping, "I can't breathe," the gang member guarding him would have opened the trunk. Then if he'd come out with a roar, taking the guy by surprise, he could have almost certainly overpowered him and run for help. Or, and possibly even better, he could have pretended that the time he had spent in the trunk had a detrimental effect on his emphysema, and he needed a doctor or a hospital or at least supplemental oxygen, fast. Once again, he was limited only by his imagination. Once out of the trunk, he could have explained that his date had leukemia, diabetes, anything, and that the excitement could cause her to go into a coma and eventually die. He could have done a thousand things if he'd kept his cool, his emotional stability, if he'd cared. Yes, cared. I don't see how he could have. After all, he was hearing his girl crying and moaning and he did nothing. Nothing. With any of the previous suggestions, chances are, the assaulters would have left, abandoning their sport, leaving the woman alone. They wouldn't want to wait around to give their regards to the police.

It is not only the man who makes the mistakes or is the object of the vendetta. In one case that was reported to me several months ago a husband and wife entered their vacation cottage after a long absence, to be welcomed by a surly gang of young toughs who had broken in a week or so earlier and were "camping" there.

While her husband was unloading the car, the wife walked up to the cottage and unlocked the front door. Several of the young toughs responded to the "intrusion" with obscenities. The woman told them to get out and furthermore that she "was not used to such language." Two members of the gang quickly grabbed her and tied and gagged her. When the husband came in, they overpowered him and tied him also.

Then they untied the woman and began taunting and fondling her. She screamed at them to leave her alone and one of the gang responded by saying that he wanted her to perform fellatio with him. She said, "I would never do that to any man. Not even my husband." They asked the husband if this was true. And at his confirmation, they forced her to have fellatio with her husband. Their comments were, "Now you won't feel so high and mighty."

In this case, the gang was determined to "punish" the woman, not her husband. It should be noted that this behavior is not unusual. Very often it is not actual penetration of the vagina which is forced upon the woman, but other sexual behavior which many victims find worse than rape.

In another case I'm acquainted with, a young couple was making out in a rose garden on the campus of a small Southeastern college. Four men from a nearby college were secretly watching—and drinking. The further the young couple went, the more excited the secret watchers got. Finally, they couldn't stand it anymore. One of them burst through the bushes, quickly followed by his companions. The eager one grabbed the woman by the arm. The woman's date knocked the man's arm away. Then he found himself surrounded. One of the men in the gang smashed him in the jaw and put him down—but not out. He lay there, ignored, while the men raped the woman again and again until they were bored with her. Her date never uttered a word, never attempted to stop them, never attempted to run for help. Fortunately for the women of the world, not every escort is as brainless or timid as this one was.

In another case I know of, the man did a fine job of protecting his date when suddenly a gang of perhaps fifteen young men came running at them. Now, this man was no pushover. He was six two and weighed two hundred and ten pounds. He had just begun a course in self-defense karate the day before. Even so, he made no attempt to stand and fight. He took hold of his date's arm and they started to run. But they couldn't run fast enough.

The man lifted his date over some bushes and told her to take off. Then he turned to face the onrushing gang. As best he could remember afterward, he managed to take out three or four of them. But the rest kept coming. Even worse, some jumped the bushes to chase his date.

He turned and ran after them, knocking them down as he overtook them and caught up with her. Knowing there was no way he could hold them all off, and knowing all too well what they wanted, he threw his date to the ground and leaped on top of her.

The gang surrounded them and beat, kicked, cut and clubbed him. But they couldn't dislodge him. Finally, they left. The man ended up with several broken ribs. And he needed more than two hundred stitches to close his wounds. The woman was totally unscathed. She didn't even have a black-and-blue mark.

As far as I'm concerned, this man did just about everything right, given the circumstances. His first reaction was to try to get both of them away from the gang, to flee, to avoid a confrontation. If he'd been successful, that would have been the end of that. When he saw that tactic wasn't going to work, he tried to get his date to safety. That might well have worked. It should have removed the temptation, so far as the gang was concerned, and freed his mind to concentrate on defending himself. But the situation didn't allow it. Finally, he took the only course left to him. He prevented the gang from getting to his friend by interposing his own body. That worked, perhaps in part because it prevented her from screaming and struggling and thereby sexually arousing her assaulters any more than they already were.

Unfortunately, in another, similar case the assaulters were also of a different ethnic group. And the woman *told* them she couldn't stand it if they touched her. They touched her, all right, and she paid dearly for her prejudices, her lack of tact and her unadulterated stupidity.

Group rape is no simple problem. If you're alone, you can divide and conquer. That will take all of your skill, judgment and imagination, but it's worth the effort, since the prize is your life, good health and peace of mind. If you're with someone (man or woman), disassociate yourself from your friend if he or she is behaving unwisely or antagonistically or see that one of you gets to safety—and help—then divide and conquer your assaulters. If you're in the dating environment, take common-sense precautions.

Should these prove fruitless, avoid the confrontation if possible, make sure one of you gets to safety—and help—then handle the situation as you would if you were by yourself.

And remember the basic rules and principles of assault prevention. Keep your head; retain your emotional stability. Don't antagonize or commit your behavior or do anything that could hurt you. Treat each assaulter as a human being, as a man not a monster. Gain his or their confidence. Go along until you can safely react. Use your imagination and your good judgment. And *all* these rules apply to any man who is about to assault you.

Of course, if you find yourself in immediate danger of your life or severe bodily harm, try anything action-oriented. In that case, and in that case only, as your last resort, fight like a tiger.

10

A Woman's Home
Is Her Castle

Not once, in the ten years I've been lecturing, has someone failed to ask, "Where am I most likely to get raped, Mr. Storaska? And is there anything special I can do to protect myself in particular locations?"

There are two places to worry about: at home or away. That's not a joke. Many women are raped in their own homes or in transit to them. In fact, I estimate that between 20 and 30 percent of all rapes occur in the victim's home and that the majority of such rapes are probably committed by total strangers. Many other authorities' statistics are higher than mine here, but this again reflects their dependence on police files. Cases like these are more readily reported and believed by police, since no one can say the women were some place they shouldn't have been and "asking for it."

Most of the rapes committed by a stranger in a person's own house can be prevented by a few simple, common-sense precautions. The solution to the problem is simple enough: keeping the rapist out.

Of course you know the obvious: keep doors and windows locked whether you're home or not; leave lights on in more than one room in the house to give the impression you're not alone; change the locks when you move into a new house or apartment. But there are some effective methods of preventing entry that might not have occurred to you.

In the first place, probably the most effective thing you can do is to contact the crime-prevention unit of your local police department. Such units are being strenghtened throughout the country, and in many instances their members are receiving excellent training from the National Crime Prevention Institute at the University of Louisville.

Men from these special units of your police department will come to your home, make a survey right on the spot, and give you free expert advice on how to safeguard the premises.

There are some basic things you can do yourself. If your home or apartment has a door without a window, have a locksmith install what's called an "interviewer." That's a little peephole with a wide-angle lens that lets you see who is knocking on your door or ringing your bell. Make sure any door leading to the outside is either solid wood (*not* the prefabricated hollow type) or the ribbed steel found in many apartments today. In addition, all outside doors should have large spring steel hinges on the inside of the door.

If your door does have windows, especially if the windows are situated so that anyone breaking them can reach through and unlock the door, get what's called a double-cylinder lock. That's the kind that has a keyhole on both the inside and the outside of the lock. (Most key locks have a turn bolt on the inside.) Hang the key on a hook near enough to the door so that you can open it quickly from the inside if you need to—if the house is on fire, for example—but not so near that an intruder can reach it if he breaks the door window or any other window nearby. *Every* door to your house that has good-sized windows should be so equipped.

You don't have to use double-cylinder locks if your doors have no windows, or if the windows are small, less than nine inches in diameter, and high. And don't worry about someone getting through such a window. Anyone who's tiny enough to get through one of these small, decorative windows can be stomped on, at your leisure.

Whether you're putting single- or double-cylinder locks on your doors, make sure they're of the "dead-bolt" or "dead-fall" type. Dead-bolt locks have a flat rectangular piece of metal that protrudes from the lock and goes into the doorjamb. Dead-fall locks have a cylindrical piece of steel that falls into three circular pieces of steel in the frame when the door is closed. They can both be jimmied, all right, but it takes time, noise, skill, and/or muscle. Most housebreakers want to get in quickly and easily, which is why these locks are effective. Although the spring latch locks that use a triangular wedge of metal can be opened by the rankest amateur in about three seconds with no tools other than a credit card, probably 90 percent of the homes in America employ this type of lock.

Most authorities recommend that you install a chain lock on your doors so that you can open the door partway to see who's knocking or ringing. I think chain locks are dangerous because there's not a man born of woman so pitifully weak that he couldn't break the average chain lock with one good shove. (Almost every woman who was strangled by the Boston Strangler had a chain lock.) The weakest point is the bracket, usually held on by short sheet metal screws, that goes into the doorjamb.

This problem of weakness can be partly alleviated by installing an angle bracket that goes around the side of the jamb and the front and attaches with long, heavy screws. But few locksmiths bother to use such brackets and they don't come with the prepackaged do-it-yourself chain locks.

Even when they're strengthened, I'm against chain locks. With them, when you open the door to determine the identity of your caller or to receive a package, you expose anywhere from one to three inches of your body, and if you're relaxing, what you are wearing may tease or entice the man on the outside. It may trigger him into using every last bit of his strength or his wit to get that door opened. (And it may surprise you to know that his wit is more effective than his strength.) Even worse, though the door is open only a few inches, there may be room enough for him to use a weapon.

Instead of a chain lock, use one of those peepholes to establish the identity of your caller. Don't open the door to accept packages. Tell the messenger or mailman to leave the package in front of the door, and you'll get it later. If he wants you to sign for it, ask him to slip the paper under the door or come back later when someone else is home. The best tactic of all: when you hear a knock on the door or your doorbell rings, call out loudly when you approach the door, "That's all right, Jack. I'll get it." I've heard of many instances where the man knocking has said after hearing such a remark, "Sorry, I have the wrong apartment."

I suppose it goes without saying that you shouldn't leave a key hidden under the doormat or in some other obvious spot outside your house. An assaulter's imagination isn't necessarily inferior to yours. And of course you should ask for identification when a repairman visits. Have him slip it under the door. When you're sure he's who he says he is, *then* open the door, not before. When in doubt, have the man wait outside while you give his company a call.

Incidentally, even the proper identification isn't any guarantee the man won't assault you. If he's thinking of murdering you, it won't matter whether or not you know his name and where he works. And there's nothing about working for the telephone company or the electric company that insures a man's emotional stability. Your best bet is to take sensible precautions. If you're alone, tell the man he can't come in. (But don't say you're alone. Instead, you might tell him that your husband or boyfriend is asleep.) Then set a time when you know you won't be by yourself.

With the proper locks it is possible to pretty well rape-proof and burglar-proof an apartment, so long as it isn't on the first floor of the apartment building and so long as you *use* the locks you have.

A house presents a more difficult problem. Almost wherever you look, it has that fragile clear stuff called glass. Windows, not doors, are a house's most vulnerable spots. Don't think you're safe if your windows have those turn-clasp locks and you keep them locked. All an intruder has to do is to break the windowpane directly above or below such a lock, flip it open, pull the window up and step inside.

The solution is something I call window wedges. These are simply hardwood wedges mounted on the upper half of a window on the inside of the frame. Properly installed, with long, strong wood screws, and placed four or five inches above the top of the bottom half of the window, they allow you to open the window to catch cool breezes while preventing it from being opened far enough for anyone to enter.

Some homeowners swear by an alarm system, either the type intended to scare an intruder and warn the occupant, or the more costly type that is connected with the police department. On the other hand, many people find an alarm system's cost prohibitive and their care a nuisance, since most of the time it's the forgetful homeowner who sets off the alarm.

You can negate every one of these precautions by walking out of your house for five or ten minutes and not locking up—a typical mistake. That doesn't demonstrate your confidence in the safety of your neighborhood. It demonstrates lack of caution, caution that is unfortunately necessary today.

If you're a woman who lives alone, there's one last hint I can offer you. Don't list your name, either in the phone book or on your mailbox, in such a way that it's obvious you're a woman. List it as S. R. Smith instead of Susan Smith. If you put your name on your mailbox, consider writing S. R. "Ox" Smith. Your friends will be amused. Your potential assaulter will be put off.

If you've taken every precaution, or if you haven't, and someone has broken into your house, you still have several alternatives. If you have a room in your house with a good, strong, solid door (not one of those hollow types) that also is equipped with a strong lock, you can lock yourself in. I recommend that you fix one room just this way, for that purpose. Make sure it's a room with an extension phone in it or, better, an extra phone with a separate number altogether, so that you can call for help.

If you can get to a phone either in that safe room or if the intruder is still in the process of breaking in, first call the police. But if there's any reasonable doubt the police will arrive in time to help you, next *call the fire department*. They *will* be there, promptly. In some localities this may be construed as a false alarm, but I consider the legal risk worth it under these circumstances. Then call the rescue squad. Then call your husband or boyfriend.

The fire department will arrive very quickly and that

should do the job. Can you imagine an assaulter persisting while six men are running up the sidewalk with axes in their hands?

Bear in mind that you should call the fire department only if it is a genuine emergency.

In one case I'm familiar with, a baby-sitter was taking care of a two-year-old when an intruder broke into the house. She immediately called the police, but the sergeant who picked up the phone evidently thought that the young woman was the same person who'd called a few days earlier, saying she was lonely and wanted him to come over. He decided not to take any action. Meanwhile the assaulter grabbed a can opener, held it to the baby's throat and forced the baby-sitter to have sexual intercourse with him, using the child as a sort of hostage. If you have time for only one phone call, still call the police, but tell them to call the fire department for you, because the fire is spreading fast to other houses. Make sure you give adequate and accurate directions.

Another alternative: if an intruder breaks into your house, get out. While he's coming in the front door, you can be going through the back door, or vice versa. Head for the nearest lighted house and ask whoever is inside to call the police. If there are no lighted houses around, head for the woods or some other dark area. He won't find you. Whatever else the assaulter may be, he isn't a bloodhound.

If you take all available precautions, if you're unable to retreat to a "safe" room, get out of the house or call for help—don't panic. Just handle the intrusion as you would any assault by a stranger. If the intruder is only after your valuables, your best course of action would be to do nothing. Above all, don't try to play heroine. If you do, the likely result is that you'll turn a burglary into a rape or assault or even possibly something worse. Remember, the burglar's main goal is to steal, then vanish. He wants no confrontation, and is probably one of the most timid of all criminals. Like the rapist, the burglar is scared and potentially explosive.

You already know my opinion of weapons, and I hope you share it. I don't advocate them under any circumstances. But if you insist on having a weapon or your husband insists that you do, your home and your car are the only two places where it might logically be useful because you can probably get to it before an attacker gets to you.

The only weapon worth talking about is a handgun. I'd rather you went out and got yourself a bazooka or a flamethrower, but those weapons, though they'd do the job, aren't exactly practical. Knives or billy clubs or other short-range weapons are worse than useless, since an assaulter can too easily take them from you and use them against you.

If you feel the absolute need to have a revolver, check first with the local law-enforcement authorities about whether or not it's legal for you to own such a weapon, whether you need a permit, license, etc. Many a woman has used a handgun or other illegal weapon on an intruder only to find *herself* arrested. If you still want a handgun, go to the training officer of your local police department and ask him to teach you how to shoot one. And then ask yourself if you'd be willing and able to use it against an intruder.

Most important, do not become dependent on any weapon. Being confident at home because you have a revolver will undermine any confidence you develop away from home, or away from your revolver. And if the temptation to carry it overcomes you—well, read Chapter 3 again.

Even Moving Targets Get Raped

The automobile is one of the most vicious weapons of the twentieth century. In this country alone it kills more than fifty thousand people a year in accidents.

There is the additional peril that certain assaulters will prey on lone women driving cars. They do this either by trying to actually ram a woman's car with theirs, or by driving beside it, edging it off the road.

This sort of thing isn't common. But over a period of ten years several hundred cases of assault via automobile have been reported to me. Still, if you keep your wits about you, you're safe from such assaults—*as long as your car is in running order.*

Suppose you're driving through a small town in the middle of the night when some man pulls up alongside you in his car and starts ramming you, trying to force you to stop.

This is exactly what happened in one case. The first time the man rammed Sara's car she thought, My God, what a stupid driver! He just ran into me. That illusion was quickly dispelled. When she slowed down, with the thought of exchanging names, addresses and insurance-company information with the other driver, he rammed her again, this time from behind.

He's a drunk, she thought. Or he's on drugs. I'd better drive on. Pretty soon, he was beside her again. Once more he rammed her. She tried to outrun him, but he caught up and rammed her again. This time she caught a glimpse of his face. He was smiling at her and motioning for her to pull over.

If I can just get home, she told herself, then Frank will help me. She kept repeating this thought in her mind again and again. As it happened, her home was only about three miles away. She sped toward it, her assaulter close behind.

When she got to her house, she pulled sharply into her driveway—and her heart sank. Frank's car was gone. She glanced at her house, then back at the assaulter, who had turned onto her block and was approaching her driveway about fifty feet away.

Since I heard about this case six years ago I've often asked women what Sara should have done. Should she have stayed in the car or should she have gone into the house? Most of the time, my audience tells me she should have gone into the house. They say she could have locked out the assaulter, then called the police.

That's wrong. A man desperate enough to ram a woman's car wouldn't be stopped by a locked door. He'd break in. And chances are, she wouldn't have time to lift the phone off the hook. And possibly she wouldn't even make it inside the house.

One of the safest places a woman can be, in a situation of this sort, is in her car, if it's still in running condition. Sara had heard my lecture, but all she could remember about this type of assault was that she should "do something weird" and "attract attention" and to stay *inside* the car and *keep* the motor *on*.

Sara did something weird and she did attract attention. She drove off her driveway and took off across her neighbors' lawns, breaking through shrubbery, knocking over small trees, crunching bicycles and, in general, making one hell of a racket and one hell of a mess. It was nearly midnight by this time, and all the neighbors were in bed. Can you imagine how they felt when they saw a pair of headlights go by the bedroom window when they knew the road was on the other side of the house?

Within about three seconds, no fewer than eighteen people came running out of their houses to see what the devil was going on. Several had already called the police. Seeing the attention she'd gained, Sara knew it was time to stop. She pulled up in front of a birdbath and got out of her car. Her assaulter could be seen driving away at high speed, perhaps afraid of being apprehended, perhaps terrified that this nut was going to turn her car around and head for him.

Fortunately, the woman was well and favorably known among her neighbors. They believed her story. But even if they hadn't it would have been all right. When you're in danger of being assaulted, raped or worse, *anything* is all right if it will work, as long as no innocent bystanders are harmed.

Later, I talked to Sara's husband, who commended her for her quick thinking. "You know," he told me, "that little drive through the neighborhood did about twenty-five hundred dollars' worth of damage. But it was worth it." I think he meant that. Of course, she was standing right there beside him when he said it and you don't mess around with somebody like Sara.

I do think Sara could have stopped the assault earlier,

though, by heading back toward town, instead of deeper and deeper into quiet, isolated suburbs. Once among other occupied cars, she could have attracted attention by driving up on the sidewalk or doing something else unusual.

She could have driven to the police station. And I don't mean she should have parked outside, then run in for help. Women have been assaulted on the steps of police precincts, hospitals, rescue stations, fire stations—places where there are people twenty-four hours a day. She should have driven right up the steps at three or four miles an hour and knocked on the precinct door with her bumper. Pretty soon, the desk sergeant would have come out and said, "Aha, we have trouble here."

Such a tactic, it's true, may damage your car, but it will protect you. And we both know which one of you is replaceable and which one isn't. By the way, don't just park outside the precinct and jam your hand on the horn. As far as the assaulter is concerned, that's exactly like screaming. He could break into your car and throttle you before the police respond. It might work, but what I'm telling you *will* work.

If you can't find a police station, a fire station or rescue house will do. And if you can't find one of those, drive in—and that's just what I mean—to an all-night drugstore, gas station or grocery. If there are no stores open in your part of the country at that hour of the night, drive up on the sidewalk and sideswipe a few store windows. Make noise. Attract attention. If you can find a jewelry store, so much the better. They have loud alarms that go off when the windows are broken. Don't hurt yourself. Drive at only a couple of miles an hour into these buildings. But drive *in*.

Another good tactic is to look for a police car and have an accident with it—hopefully a small one. I can think of nothing more likely to convince your assaulter that he should buzz off in another direction.

The newspapers recently printed a story about a Brooklyn nurse who was accosted in the lobby of her apartment building by a big man who said he had a gun in his pocket. He forced her to accompany him to the roof of the building, she told the police, where he raped her, then robbed her of sixteen dollars.

While searching her purse for money, he found the car keys. After the attack he forced her to drive him around Brooklyn for more than an hour. The terrified woman finally spotted a police radio car at the intersection of Tompkins Avenue and Van Buren Street and rammed it.

The rapist attempted to flee on foot, but the nurse screamed: "Grab him! He raped me!" Police Officer William Russel, who was alone in the radio car, collared the suspect and brought him back to the precinct house, where he was charged with rape, sodomy, kidnapping and robbery.

It's all well and good to attract attention, to drive into a police station or other occupied building or to knock fenders with a police car, so long as you're in or near town. If the assault by automobile takes place in the country, remember the auto-assault rule: your car is the safest place you can be, so long as it's in running condition. Be aware that if someone tries to force you off the road at high speed, you are in immediate danger of your life or severe bodily harm and anything goes.

What you have to do, for your own safety, is to stop the assault as quickly and as permanently as possible. Though the assaulter may get a charge out of ramming you and frightening you, his main conscious motive is to touch you, to get his hands on you, to rape you. That can't happen if both of you stay in your cars.

So pull off to the shoulder as quickly as possible and stop the car. *But leave the engine running.* If he really wants to assault you, he'll pull up in front of you, probably angling his car so that you're at least partially blocked from going back on the road. Then he'll get out and start toward you.

When he gets within, say, ten feet or so, back up—he'll run toward you—then put the car into forward and run into him. Then back up and go around his car if you can, or back up and turn around and drive to town and get an ambulance and call the police.

You don't need to grind him into the pavement. Just give him a light tap, at about five miles an hour. That will smash his knees. When the police get there he'll still be around.

Even if the car is full of men, all of them coming out after you, you don't have to worry about it. Just knock one down and the rest will see the merits of caution. They'll end up cowering behind their car.

One of the worst nightmares that women have is that they'll be surrounded by a motorcycle gang. But, so long as you stay in your car, keep the doors locked and keep moving, whatever happens, it will happen to *them*, not you. Motorcycles aren't worth a darn against a car. A motorcycle can crash into your car at full tilt and do nothing more than make a big dent. But all you have to do is tap a motorcycle with your bumper and the rider will go sprawling.

If—and it's not very likely—you're ever surrounded by a motorcycle gang when you're in your car, don't let their appearance frighten you too much. They're trying to look as if they're on leave from hell, but underneath the helmets and black leather jackets, they're people—nothing more, nothing less. Should they start to come for you, put your car in drive, put it in reverse, swing the steering wheel from side to side, and watch the motorcycles fly through the air.

These are the tactics to use if you're ever assaulted while

driving alone in your car. But it would be much better to take some simple precautions that can stop most such attacks before they start.

In a parking lot the first thing to do is make sure you're not attacked while you're *on your way* to your car. Some rapists prowl the unlighted edges of big shopping-center parking lots, or dark parking lots behind a row of shops, hoping to find a lone woman to victimize.

A rapist may follow you to your car, jump you, force you inside and drive off with you. You can foil that maneuver by parking close to the store, even if you have to wait a few minutes for a place, or, if that's impossible, by parking under a bright parking-lot light. If you have some distance to walk, on the way back to your car, have the manager or a clerk either go along with you or watch you from the store. Get your key out when you're still in the store. Don't stand at your car door fumbling in your purse. This goes for entering your house also. Open the door, get in, lock up.

A rapist may also wait for you *inside your own car*, in the back seat, perhaps after having watched you park. If you lock up when you leave your car, that's not likely to happen. Just to be sure, make it a habit to check your back seat before getting into your car. If you see someone, walk on as if you didn't. Get help.

Once you're in your car, keep your doors locked and your windows rolled up, to prevent anyone on foot from getting into your car before you know what's happening— such as at a stoplight or a stop sign. If it's hot, use the air conditioner, or open your windows a crack.

If you're frequently out in your car alone at night, put a bag of groceries, a bundle of laundry or a big stuffed animal on the passenger seat and put a man's hat on it. Ninety-nine times out of a hundred, a potential assaulter will think you have company. The other time he'll think you're some kind of nut. Either way, you're safe.

If you're out late and you're driving home, let someone know when you're leaving, when to expect you and what route you're taking. That way, if you're unusually late, at least someone will know where to start looking.

Don't take the scenic route if it's late at night or if the scenic route takes you through a bad neighborhood. The same goes for the shortcut. If possible, take the main highway, so that you have plenty of company and lots of light. Even if it takes a few minutes longer, it's the safer way.

Check your gas tank before every trip. Running out is not only embarrassing, it's dangerous.

Learn how to fix a flat tire, if you don't already know how, and try it at least once. A flat tire can seem like a disaster if you don't know how to change it, but it's a fairly simple ten-minute job if you know what you're doing. It's only common sense to keep your spare tire in good shape, of course. If this is too much trouble, equip your car with steel-belted radial tires. They're the type least likely to have punctures.

Make sure your car is well-maintained. Keep it tuned up, oiled, lubricated. I don't know much about cars, but I do know that you can avoid almost every breakdown with preventive maintenance.

If, despite such precautions, you're alone in your car and you have a breakdown at night on a lonely road, should you stay inside or get out?

Usually, when I ask this question, almost everybody in the audience says you should stay inside. They're wrong. A car may be the safest place for you when it's in running condition, but there's nothing particularly safe about it when it's broken down. It doesn't matter if you keep the doors locked and the windows rolled up. All an assaulter has to do is pick up a rock or take off his shoe, smash a side window, unlock the door and pull you out. Car-window glass is shatterproof—*not* breakproof.

(I can see only one exception to this rule: if you're driving through a dangerous neighborhood and your car breaks down, I'd advise staying with your car, even if it won't run, locking the doors, rolling up the windows, and hiding on the floor. Stay there until rush hour or until nearby stores are open, or until other help arrives. It will, especially if you've told someone your route and expected time of arrival. But instead of going through all this, why not just take some other, safe route?)

If you're in a secluded area and your car breaks down, get out, lift up the hood and trunk, open all the doors, turn on the lights, tie a handkerchief on the aerial, tie down the horn if you can (making it blow) and generally turn your vehicle into something resembling a neon light or its close equivalent. You are blatantly asking for help.

Then take the flashlight and blanket you always keep in the trunk for emergencies like these and get off the road about thirty to fifty steps and hide. If there are woods nearby, so much the better. Step in a few paces, so that you can see your car but a person on the road can't see you. Don't worry about the woods. The chance that a rapist or anyone else is lurking among the trees is about as close to zero as you can get. If there's no cover, kneel or lie down. No one will suspect you're there.

Someone will come along after a while, stop and take a look at your car. While they're doing that, you take a look at them. A car full of drunks is a guarantee of more trouble. A state trooper is perfect. Though assaulters have been known to impersonate policemen, almost always anyone who represents a law enforcement officer will be legit. A man, his wife and six children of assorted ages is another good choice.

The point is that if you're outside the car, you get to

choose who helps you. If you're inside, your helper gets to choose you. You have to take the first person to come along.

In nine hundred and ninety-nine cases out of a thousand, anyone you ask for help will willingly give it to you. But if there's one chance in a thousand that you'll get assaulted and raped instead, it's not worth taking. You may be uncomfortable if you follow this advice. You may waste time. But you'll have time to waste, because you'll still be around.

If your car breaks down, the temptation to hitchhike home or back to town will be enormous. Don't yield to it. Walk. And when a car comes along, get back off the road, out of sight. If I were a woman and I wanted to get raped right now, if I didn't have any time to fool around, I'd hitchhike. Perhaps it won't happen the first time, but if you hitchhike at the same place and the same time for a week or ten days, the chances are excellent for getting raped.

Several years ago I took a poll of two hundred and fifty men, fifty on each of five campuses in five different parts of the country. I asked them one question: if you're riding along in a car and you see a woman hitchhiking alone at night, what goes through your mind? Nearly 90 percent said that if they wanted to do something to her, she'd be very easy. (And I didn't ask this question in the context of sex or assaults.) Most of the rest said that if they *didn't* do something to her, she'd be disappointed. "She's asking for it," was a common way of putting it.

The striking thing about this poll is that it was taken not of convicted rapists or sex criminals or dirty old men but of college men, who probably hitchhiked often enough themselves and therefore should have had empathy for a woman who hitchhiked, and who were full participants in the contemporary lifestyle.

Imagine the results if I'd ask the same question of two

hundred and fifty men in their late thirties or early forties, say, who hadn't hitchhiked for years, if ever, who were taught that women didn't do such things, who looked with envy at what they perceived to be the "liberated sexuality" of the younger generation.

Remember, many, many men perceive women as sexual objects, in addition to however else they view them. When such a man sees what he perceives to be a sex object making herself easily available, apparently teasing, making advances herself, it's no surprise that he has sexual thoughts and that he sometimes carries these thoughts through to the conclusion logical to him.

Women hitchhikers get raped and sometimes even murdered. (And so do men hitchhikers.)

Last winter and fall, eight young women, most of them college students, were murdered while hitchhiking. At least two dozen others in the college communities between Cambridge and Boston were sexually assaulted while hitchhiking during the same period.

Since May 1972 five college coeds believed to be hitchhiking between home and campus in the Santa Cruz, California, area, south of San Francisco, have been found brutally slain and two others are still missing. In the first three months of 1973, eleven other young women from that area were raped while hitchhiking.

In the last couple of years, seven teenagers and young women, from age thirteen to twenty-three, have been raped and murdered in the Ann Arbor–Ypsilanti, Michigan, area after accepting rides from strangers.

At a university in Southern California, there were a hundred and twelve reported rapes connected with hitchhiking in a recent nine-month period. A university in Colorado experienced a hundred and twenty reported rapes connected with hitchhiking in a single year's time. We don't know how many took place that weren't reported, but it's a safe bet there were plenty.

Some men look for hitchhikers as they drive by colleges or high schools. They pick up a coed looking for a ride from her psychology class to her sociology class and assault her. Others may drive alongside a woman waiting for a bus, ask for directions to some street on the bus line, and then, as a seemingly casual afterthought, offer the woman a lift—then rape her. For other men, there's no premeditation involved. It's just a matter of opportunity. And these men needn't be "older." They can be young, mod or hippie, have long hair or short, dressed Ivy League or bush.

After I gave a lecture at a large university in Michigan one day, a woman came up to me and told me that she'd hitchhiked and been molested. "Just about the first thing the man did was stick his hand in my pants. When I protested, he told me, 'Go ahead and report it, baby. You're the one who hitchhiked, not me.'"

For a large part of society, the part that disapproves of the sexual revolution, free spirits and experimental lifestyles, that man had a point. He was saying that by hitchhiking the woman had voluntarily placed herself in a compromising position. The majority of our society interprets hitchhiking as an invitation—whether it is or not. Because of that, when a woman hitchhikes, not only does she put herself in line for rape, but she also severely damages her legal defenses against her assaulter. When a woman is raped while hitchhiking, a Clarence Darrow would have a hard time getting her assaulter convicted.

I would like our society, especially the male contingent, to consider that a woman hitchhiker may not want to be raped. As a matter of fact, she may not want to be made love to. She may simply want to get to another place, to her destination. Understood?

I know that hitchhiking in many areas is a matter of

custom, tradition, transportation and hospitality. It galls me to have to say it, but I'm afraid that in this case you can't act on your impulse to trust other people. Under *no* circumstances should you hitchhike. The risk simply isn't worth the few minutes or the few pennies you think you're going to save. I know the temptation is enormous, especially when you need to go from one end of campus to another and you only have five minutes to do it. But if you yield to that temptation, you're tempting the man who picks you up—and you're tempting fate.

I also include "hitchhiking by appointment," which is what I call answering an ad on a college bulletin board from a guy who's driving to California on the fourteenth and wants a rider to share expenses and driving. Unless you know him or you can, and do, find out about him, you may be risking your body, your mind, or even your life. Colleges and universities should require a person placing such an ad to identify himself to the authorities before the trip.

It is unsafe to hitchhike alone *and* unsafe if you're in a group, *or* with your boyfriend. If you're with two other women and your driver has a weapon, he can pick up all three of you, have a good time with each, then dispose of you one at a time.

As for hitchhiking with your boyfriend, I've studied thirty-four separate cases where the women ended up raped. What happened in every instance was that her boyfriend, being polite but not too smart, let the woman get into the car first. Then the car drove away before he could join her.

I don't think even men should hitchhike. There's been a substantial increase in the number of assaults on men: sexual assaults, robberies, simple brutality. A man isn't in as much danger as a woman, but that doesn't mean he should hitchhike.

The same goes for picking up hitchhikers, which is no different from hitching yourself. And the same holds for a man. In recent days a racket has developed in which either young girls or boys hitch rides, then threaten the man they're riding with by saying they intend to leap out of the car at the next intersection and say they've been molested unless the man gives them two dollars or five dollars or whatever. This isn't rape, but it is a kind of sexual attack. How should you handle it? The best way is by not picking up a hitchhiker in the first place. But if you do and this happens to you, drive directly to the nearest police station. Go in and report the incident. Chances are, the little extortionists will have long since run away. If not, the very fact that *you*, not they, have reported the incident will put the law on your side.

Hitchhiking is a particularly dangerous game for children. Parents should forbid it absolutely. More than that, they should know exactly what sort of transportation their children *will* have to and from wherever it is they're going. When in doubt, they should provide transportation. And they should be especially wary when their child says he'll walk. He may intend to hitchhike.

Hitchhiking is nothing less than roulette by automobile. And it's not a matter of judgment. You have no way of knowing if the man who picks you up will rape you. You have no way of knowing the man or woman, boy or girl, you pick up won't cause some kind of serious trouble for you. It's depressing to say that you can't trust your fellow human beings—and probably in almost every instance you can. But a mistake can be disastrous.

If nothing else will convince you, consider this: every year, some nine hundred people die while hitchhiking, not because they're murdered by an assaulter but because they're *hit* by cars.

I wish I could tell you that if, forsaking hitchhiking or

cars, you always walked where you were going instead, you'd be safe from rape. Not so. A large percentage of all rapes occur or start on the street.

Sometimes such an attack takes place without warning. You have no time to react, to take preventive measures. There's no way to avoid a confrontation. In that case, you must deal with your assaulter by following the laws of assault safety and the rules of rape prevention. If necessary, use what you've learned here about physical self-defense. You're hardly helpless.

If you're walking down the sidewalk at night alone in a secluded neighborhood and you see a man or group of men following you or approaching you, don't walk on fearlessly. Looking brave brings on the same problems as screaming, running or struggling. What you should do, immediately, is cross the street, as if your destination were on the other side. And do it while there's as much distance between you as possible. This tactic gives you time to think, time to look around the neighborhood and spot the lighted houses, time to size up the situation. It also at least partially removes what may be tempting your potential assaulter or assaulters —you.

Crossing the street under these circumstances is a test. If the man or men continue on, without crossing to meet you, they've passed the test. If they cross they've failed. In that case, go immediately to the nearest lit house, as if it's your destination, ring the doorbell, push the buzzer, knock with the knocker and say, "Mom, Dad, Moose—I'm home." Say it loud enough for anyone following you to hear.

When someone comes to the door, if it's obvious that you're in danger of assault, ask them to call a cab for you, or to call your father, husband, boyfriend or the police. If you're not so sure, just ask, "Does Suzy Smith live here?" The answer to that will be no, of course, and you may feel like an idiot for asking the question. But just the fact that you've made contact with someone else may be enough to convince your assaulter or assaulters to keep on walking.

If you get no answer at the nearest lit house and you're reasonably sure there's someone inside, bend down, pick up a rock or take off your shoe and heave it through the living-room window. That will get a response, I guarantee you. It may also bring the police—and what's wrong with that?

If there is no answer, go to the next lit house. If there are no lit homes around or if you can't get anyone to come to the door, turn and face your assaulter or assaulters and get ready to deal with the situation. All is not lost. That's what we've been talking about all this time.

I want to emphasize one thing here: most of the time when a man comes up to you on the street, he won't do anything. He may make some kind of remark or say something vulgar. In that case, act as though you didn't hear him. (This is different from ignoring him, by the way.) Treat the language as if it's nothing unusual. Nine times out of ten, if the man does do something he'll do nothing more than *touch* you. Don't react antagonistically. Bad language directed your way or even a momentary touch is essentially harmless. If you react antagonistically you could make the situation dangerous.

By the way, everything I've said about walking goes for bicycling. You're no safer on a bicycle than you are on foot. Thinking that you are is a common error. For that reason, you'd be wise never to bicycle anywhere or anytime you wouldn't be willing to walk. Additionally, whether you walk to work or use some sort of transportation, it is wise to consider varying your schedule so that you are not leaving and arriving at exactly the same time every day. This is especially important if it is nighttime during any part of your trip.

Other common rape locales include public transportation and elevators. A healthy application of common sense and a reasonable amount of caution should help you avoid any assaults in these situations. But here are a few hints:

When you're taking public transportation—train, bus, subway, boat, tramp steamer, hot-air balloon or whatever —stay close to the operator. This is a good idea whether or not you're alone.

Now I've heard it advocated that every time you get off a bus, say, you should walk a few steps, then turn around to see if someone is following you. I don't think much of that idea. Sure, someone may be following you, someone who just happens to be going in the same direction as you are. But if you raise caution to that level, you're no longer merely alert, you're paranoid. If you keep looking around to see if someone is following you, someday you'll be right. He'll be wearing a white coat and white pants and he'll be carrying a net.

As for elevators, don't enter one with someone who makes you nervous. If you're already inside and such a man joins you, say, "Oh, my package" (or my umbrella or my hat) and get off. If you're caught in the elevator with such a person, and it's already moving, press the next floor button and get out. If you can't get out and he's clearly going to attack you—well, you know what to do then.

Most of all, use your common sense. Be aware of your environment.

It Takes All Kinds

Your chances of ever being raped are small, but it is almost certain that at least once in your life you will be the victim of a "minor" sexual annoyance from an obscene phone caller, an exhibitionist, a Peeping Tom, or some other sexual aberrant. A man or woman may follow you as you walk down the street, or make lewd and vulgar remarks to you as you pass by, or touch or rub against you in crowded places, or make unwelcome sexual advances.

I've used the word "minor" to describe such episodes because studies show that they rarely present any danger of rape or injury. Nonetheless, they can be extremely frightening or disturbing and will probably *seem* dangerous as they're taking place.

You should learn to deal with such situations, primarily to prevent yourself from making serious mistakes, errors that could transform an essentially harmless episode into something genuinely dangerous.

The most common type of "minor" sexual annoyance is the obscene phone call and the most common caller is the "breather," the man who gets on the telephone and does nothing but breathe loudly. If you've had one of these calls, you may not have recognized its sexual nature, but very likely the man on the other end of the line is masturbating.

Next in line in terms of frequency is the man who calls a woman and talks vulgarly. I had occasion to hear one of these phone calls on an extension phone when a detective called me in as a consultant in a case where an obscene phone caller was calling a certain woman again and again. Within an hour from the time I sat down the man called.

Until that moment, I'd felt I was unshockable when it came to dirty words, but the caller's language was so obscene and his ideas so bizarre that he not only shocked me but would have shocked anyone.

Another type of caller will never utter a nasty word. He just asks, even begs, you to talk to him—about anything. While you talk he pictures you in his mind or masturbates.

The subtlest of all is the man who calls and asks you to participate in a sex survey he's doing for a university or a magazine or even a hospital. He may give you the names of his references, possibly even including a friend of yours he's already called. He may sound extremely convincing. Once he gets you to agree, he starts asking you questions about your sex life. He may never actually talk obscenely. He may finish his questions, thank you politely and say good-by. Or his questions may get more and more suggestive until it's obvious to you that you're having an obscene telephone call, not participating in a university-sanctioned survey. (Actually, such surveys are *never* conducted by phone.)

The *modus operandi* of the obscene telephone caller may vary, but the motive is always the same. The caller is getting sexual satiation from talking to you, from hearing a woman's voice, from shocking you and humiliating you, from dominating you verbally. You are being raped, by phone.

The defense against obscene telephone calls is simple. Get off the phone. Hang up the instant you realize you're being victimized. Don't yield to the impulse to say, "You're disgusting," or, "You ought to be ashamed of yourself," or "Why don't you tell me who you are, you coward? My husband would love to know your name." Talking to the man, whatever you say, is a sexual response so far as he is concerned because yours is a woman's voice and because you're staying on the phone, talking to him. Not only are you adding to his sexual satisfaction during the call, you're reinforcing his behavior, making it likely he'll make such a call again, maybe to you, maybe to some other woman— maybe to a child who is emotionally less well equipped to deal with such assaults. I know of several cases in which an obscene telephone caller has persuaded a child to take off his or her clothing and describe the process in detail—what button is being unbuttoned and so on. Many a parent has come into a room to find his or her young child on the phone, sobbing, half dressed.

If you do manage to convince your caller you're angry, all you'll be doing is antagonizing. And if he's found your telephone number, he can also find your address. They're both on the same line in the phone book, remember? Make your obscene phone caller mad enough and you may get to meet him in person.

That's what most women worry about when they get an obscene telephone call. They wonder if the call is a prelude to a visit. Unless you've encouraged the man or angered him, the chance that he'll pay you a visit is almost nil. Only in the rarest cases has this happened, and in these cases there's been an element of doubt about whether the caller already knew the woman.

Even after a single obscene phone call, I'd advise that

you call the police and report it. Your call may be part of a larger pattern and notifying them may help them to catch the caller, though the police or the phone company probably wouldn't tap your phone if it happens only once.

If you hang up the moment you realize you're involved in an obscene phone call, you'll be giving your caller precious little gratification. The odds are he'll try another number, hoping to find a woman who will stay on the phone longer. But what if it happens again and again? This is the time to ask the police or the phone company to try to trace the call. But you needn't be idle while you wait for the bugging experts to arrive. If your "friend" calls again, don't speak to him, but don't hang up, either. Take any hard object—a ballpoint pen, a ring, a coin—and *tap* it against the part of the phone you normally talk into. Tap rhythmically, once every fifteen seconds. Say nothing. Hold the receiver away from your ear, if you want. The noise he'll hear will make him think the call is being traced.

Never shout, clap your hands loudly or blow a whistle into the phone. That's exactly the same as screaming in the event of rape. Your assaulter will be angered. He may want to shut you up. We're trying to prevent assaults, not looking for new ways to get assaulted.

Another thing you might do, if he persists in calling is to keep him on the line for a minute or so without speaking, just rhythmically tapping the metal object on the receiver, then talking not into the phone but into the room, loudly enough so he can hear. Say, "That was him, all right, Officer. Did the trace work?" This isn't antagonistic. You're not attacking the caller in any way. You're just letting him eavesdrop on your conversation with the police. It should be enough to get him to cross your number off his list. If he's angry with anyone here, it will be the police. And they can handle him.

The next technique down the scale is to tape-record a

gruff male voice using foul language, and when he calls, play it back to him over the phone. Again, you're not being antagonistic to him—that unidentified man at your number is.

In a few cases, obscene phone callers might persist despite all the ploys. If this happens to you, and the police and the phone company are unable to determine his identity, consider changing your number or even getting an unlisted number. Both will cause you inconvenience, of course, and that should be weighed against the annoyance itself. What you do depends on how you feel about the problem.

There's another sort of phone call that may mean trouble and it's not obscene at all. It's the call from "someone at work," whose voice you don't recognize and whose name you don't know, asking to talk to your husband—whether you have one or not. The object of this call may be to see if you're home alone, and if you are, the call may be followed up by robbery or assault.

Never tell anyone you don't know that you're alone in the house. Instead, say your husband can't come to the phone now, that you'll be happy to take a name and number, that he'll call back as soon as possible.

The caller may say, "When can I expect a return call?" Tell him (or her—sometimes couples work this trick together) you're not sure, but it will be as soon as possible, whenever your husband is free.

Don't be paranoid. Every voice you hear on the phone doesn't mean you harm. Just be smart. Make protective behavior a habit, but never let yourself become so hypersensitive that your behavior interferes with your right to live and be free and happy.

After obscene phone calls, the most common type of "minor" sexual annoyance is when someone rubs against you or touches you in a crowded place. The technical term for this is "frottage."

In these circumstances, women are often advised to say loudly, "Would you please get your hands off me?" This is exactly the opposite of the way she should react. It's antagonistic and embarrassing to the man and might precipitate an attack.

This is not to say that if you are on a crowded subway—with a policeman in the corner—and some meek little man is rubbing against you, you're in danger if you shout at him.

In most cases, you're in no danger whatever. That's true of all the "minor" annoyance situations. But why do anything that has even a remote possibility of making the episode explode? That's a real possibility if you react antagonistically.

Instead, move out of the situation if you can. If you're in a very crowded area, strike up a conversation with a nearby stranger: "Do you have the time?" or "Crowded in here, isn't it?" Act as if you know the person you're talking to. If your molester sees that you have help nearby and he's doing something he shouldn't be doing, he'll stop.

You might turn to your molester, smile and say, "Gosh, it's crowded in here, isn't it?" Be pleasant but be sure he understands you're not encouraging him. Pretend he meant nothing by what he was doing, that it was an accident. Treating him like a well-meaning person may help him behave like one.

On the other hand, if you act as if he's disgusting or repulsive, your contempt or disdain will inevitably show through, he'll perceive it as antagonism, and you may have trouble.

Frottage, after all, is essentially trivial. It may even be accidental. It's only a momentary unpleasantness. It isn't important enough to risk making it dangerous.

What should you do if that sort of thing happens to you? Nothing, I'd say. If there's a policeman around, I suppose you could report it. But the man who touched you is probably a harmless creature—unless antagonized. He's unlikely to commit any other type of sexual offense. Certainly you didn't want to be touched and he had no right whatever to touch you. He is completely in the wrong, but you've suffered no lasting harm and I think antagonizing him isn't worth the risk to you.

Another common "minor" sexual-annoyance situation occurs when a man follows you down the street, block after block. (I'm talking now about being followed in the daylight hours through crowded streets. If you're being followed at night in an isolated area, the annoyance could be minor, but it has a greater chance of becoming an actual physical assault.)

Probably, you've been followed several times in your life and never even realized it because there were no consequences. Perhaps the man following you wasn't in any way emotionally disturbed. He just admired you and trailed along behind you for a little while because that was the direction he was going, too. Perhaps you were followed by a man who wanted to strike up a conversation and maybe make a date—nothing much wrong with that either.

On the other hand, you may have been tailed by a compulsive follower, a man who walked along behind you for many blocks, a man who didn't want to get close to you or talk to you, but was perfectly pleased to follow and let his imagination run wild.

In some ways, it's hard to call this even a minor sexual-annoyance situation. The only thing sexual about what's happening is what the man is thinking. You're not usually in any danger from him. It would be the exception if anything more that just "following" occurred. But it's no fun to think someone is following you. For this reason, and since there is a very, very slight chance he has other things in mind, I'd advise you to break the link as soon as you know you're being followed. An easy way is to walk into a store—for example, a woman's shoe store. You might also double back, right toward him, passing him going the opposite direction.

If he's unusually persistent and you find his presence threatening, you might stop a policeman, or a store clerk, or any other man who happens to be handy, and quietly ask for directions. Your follower, if he has reason to feel guilty, will think you're talking about him. That should be enough to get him walking away from you.

Don't look for people following you. People may have completely legitimate reasons for taking exactly the route you're taking, and even if you're walking up to your own door, your follower may be nothing more than a salesman or a delivery boy. Don't go overboard with alertness. Most people who seem to be following you aren't, and those who are almost never mean you any harm.

Another minor sexual-annoyance situation you might experience involves the exhibitionist, the man who displays his genitals. Usually, he finds a place where there are plenty of young women or girls or children—a high school or college, a library, a movie house, a park, a skating rink or camp.

A typical scene involving an exhibitionist: a man in a car pulls up to a young woman or group of young women and asks for directions. They come over to his car, look in and discover that he is naked from the waist down, perhaps even masturbating.

Another typical scene with an exhibitionist would take place in a park. A man wearing a raincoat is standing behind some bushes, and as a woman walks by, he opens his raincoat and exposes himself. This type of exhibitionist is called "a flasher."

Exhibitionists are very common. Many psychologists believe that the man is symbolically attempting to demonstrate his manhood. Furthermore, he's trying to shock his victim, and through this shock, to dominate her. In that sense, exhibitionism is related to rape, though the consequences for the victim are certainly much less severe.

If you see an exhibitionist, don't try to tear him down. Don't laugh, call him names, act indignant, or tell him he should be ashamed of himself. These are all varieties of antagonism. Each of them commits your behavior. Each may make him angry.

The best thing you can do is to act as if what's happening simply isn't happening at all, or that it is completely normal and not worth making a big deal over. Your goal should be to end the encounter as quickly and quietly as possible, with no fuss. In other words, to get out of there.

Don't study the exhibitionist for identifying marks or scars, don't memorize his face, don't stay around with the thought of helping the police. You aren't in danger from this man, but you're probably having an experience that's making you quite uncomfortable and there's no reason to prolong it or, worse, risk antagonizing him. If you can identify him and you know where he is, or if you have his license number, by all means report him to the police. His exhibitionism may not be dangerous in itself, but such people have been known to molest children. They don't need imprisonment, in my view, but they do need help.

Some women are particularly distressed by exhibitionists because they feel they've been singled out. This is rarely the case. Exhibitionism, like making obscene telephone calls, is habitual, compulsive, almost random behavior. The man with this compulsion only seeks opportunities and he isn't likely to be terribly choosy about his "victim."

In a way, the exhibitionist and the obscene phone caller are doing the same thing. Both are attempting to shock their victims and thereby dominate or humiliate them. So is the man who makes vulgar remarks to a woman as she walks by him. This frequently happens at big-city construction sites where an attractive woman, walking by, is greeted by a chorus of whistles, catcalls and wisecracks, some of them vulgar or obscene.

In this sort of circumstance, the safest thing you can do, whatever you're feeling, is to keep walking. Don't react as if you're being insulted or threatened. Treat the remarks casually but don't join in or encourage the talk. Though you may really resent this sort of "flattery," don't challenge it. Don't antagonize. While you are probably in no danger in daylight with other people around, there is the chance that you will antagonize one of those men who may have special problems and incite him to take some delayed vengeance.

The Peeping Tom is, in some ways, the mirror image of the exhibitionist. He isn't interested in displaying his genitals, he wants to see someone else's. Furthermore, in most cases, he does not want to be seen himself. To his way of thinking, he takes advantage of you by looking at you against your will when you are totally unaware of his attention. Typically, the Peeping Tom looks into windows.

For most women, seeing a Peeping Tom is a frightening experience because they're unsure what the man might do next. Is he a burglar? Is he a reconnoitering rapist? Is he some kind of lunatic?

According to all the research that's been done on the subject, ninety-nine times out of a hundred, all the Peeping Tom wants to do is look at you. Still, when you spot a man peering into your window, you have no way of knowing if he is a typical Peeping Tom or if he is something more dangerous. After all, burglars do "case the joint," and the man you see may be doing just that. Rapists, too, want to know if there's a potential victim inside a house before they break in.

Call the police immediately if you see a Peeping Tom at your window. The windows and doors should already be locked, of course, but if they're not, don't run around locking them. Call the police. Once help is on the way, you can start locking up.

Ideally, you should take some precautions that will stop the Peeping Tom from ever becoming interested in you. Make sure your house has opaque shades or blinds, and use them not only when you're dressing and undressing but also when you're wearing any attire inappropriate for the street, such as a nightgown, pajamas, a negligee, underwear. The shades, blinds or drapes should be sufficiently lightproof that no one can see from the outside which room you're in. You see, to some Peeping Toms the shadow of a woman dressing or undressing is just as sexually arousing as a full view. As a matter of fact, you shouldn't be visible from the outside at *any* time.

When you open the back door of the house in the morning to get the milk or the front door to get the newspaper, at least put on a raincoat over your nightgown. I know of one milkman who made it a point to watch the doors after he delivered milk. He told me that it was practically like going to a striptease show. If he had been a true Peeping Tom—a "professional" rather than an "amateur" he would have returned to the houses of women who carelessly exhibited themselves.

Though the housewife is the main target of the Peeping Tom, and especially the housewife who lives in a one-family home, such a man also frequents college dorms or bath houses at the beach or anywhere else he's likely to see women or girls disrobe. I have studied cases where Peeping

Toms have climbed into dorms and watched women take showers, after carefully calculating when shower time was.

The classic Peeping Tom is shy, sexually underexperienced and terribly afraid of a normal relationship with a woman and of being rejected. He has so scaled down his sexual demands that a good look is all he needs to obtain sexual gratification. The literature is full of cases where a man first peeped, then raped. I don't believe that these men were Peeping Toms. They were rapists setting up their victims.

Homosexual attacks may be potentially more dangerous than the other behavior we've been discussing. I've studied more homosexual attacks by men on men than by women on women, but the principles for handling such an assault are exactly the same as with heterosexual rape. Don't antagonize, treat the assaulter as a person, go along until you can safely react, etc.

In one case I'm familiar with, a woman was walking along the street when a carload of women drove up, grabbed her and pulled her into the car. Instead of fighting or struggling with them, she simply pretended to be one of them, allowing them to touch her and touching them back. She didn't act indignant or upset. Her attackers drove on a few blocks and let her out.

To my way of thinking, she did exactly the right thing. The truth was, she was very upset by the attack, even disgusted. But she knew that if she'd revealed her attitude, that would have been very antagonistic and it might have resulted in a beating or worse.

On another level, you may be approached in the dorm, at work, or by a friend or acquaintance who is a lesbian. Should this happen and you do not desire such contact, treat the approach exactly the way you'd treat a heterosexual approach, a request for a date, because essentially that's what it is. Don't act shocked, repelled, or disgusted. Don't denounce, don't scoff or belittle. Treat the homosexual as a person, for that's what she is. Don't antagonize her.

Assuming you don't wish this sort of sexual experience, the best thing to say to a lesbian is that while you have nothing against her or her sexual preference, it just isn't what interests you. Men turn you on, not women, sexually speaking, though you enjoy having friends of both sexes. Be friendly, be accepting, but be firm.

Some women would put into the category of minor sexual annoyance transvestite behavior, where a man or woman wears clothing—especially undergarments—of the opposite sex.

Transvestites don't usually annoy anyone, but some people find the very sight of them offensive. If you feel that way, you owe it to yourself and to the transvestite not to show such feelings. If you antagonize, by showing your disgust or by laughing, you may invite violence. Like other sexual variants, the transvestite may be emotionally disturbed (if only from the abuse of an unempathetic society). Antagonism on your part could trigger an explosion on his.

After a lecture in the spring of 1970, a woman came up to the stage and said, "I had quite a different experience last month—something that I thought you would be interested to learn about." There was an attractive though bashful bachelor in her office who seemed a bit lost. After getting to know him better, she invited him over to dinner at her apartment.

The man had seemed to enjoy her company at the office, but was reluctant to accept her invitation. She insisted and he finally agreed, but he was nervous when he arrived and never really settled down. They sat and talked in the living room for a while, then she said, "Please excuse me a moment. I have to check on dinner."

"Please don't leave me!" the bachelor said, very disturbed.

The woman looked at him, puzzled, but he seemed to regain his composure. She went into the kitchen, did what needed to be done, and came back into the living room. The man wasn't there. She started to look for him, thoroughly perplexed.

"I opened my bedroom door," she told me, "and found him trying on one of my bras. He already had on a pair of my panties and a pair of my stockings. My immediate reaction was to laugh. It was the funniest thing I'd ever seen. The longer I looked, the harder I laughed. He started yelling at me. 'Stop,' he said. 'I can't help it.' But I thought it was all a joke and I kept laughing. All at once, he came at me with fists flying. When I came to, the garments of mine that he'd been wearing were on the floor beside me, torn to shreds. I was badly bruised and beaten. He was gone."

This woman did just about everything wrong. She shouldn't have had him come to her apartment before she knew him better. She should have picked up the signals he was sending out and realized that he was trying to convey something by his reluctance to go out with her. Many women have a strong tendency to pick up strays, especially if they seem helpless. They gather such shy men like nails to a magnet.

Then when she found him in her bedroom in her clothes, she shouldn't have antagonized him by laughing at him—especially after he pleaded with her. Something far more serious than the beating she suffered could have happened.

It may be easy to feel contempt or disgust for a person who commits a minor sexual annoyance. But I'm not sure it's an appropriate feeling, even if we keep it to ourselves. Every human being has within his psyche at least the seeds of all the impulses that lead to "minor" sexual-annoyance offenses—obscene calling, frottage, exhibitionism, Peeping Tom-ism, following, transvestism, even homosexuality.

For example, most young couples have engaged in some kind of love talk—romantic or sexual—by phone. Such a conversation might be considered obscene by some people.

Or take frottage, or rubbing. Every human being who enjoys close physical contact with another human being is familiar with the pleasures this activity can bring.

Even exhibitionism isn't foreign to most of us. On the beach, both men and women often show as much of their bodies as they can, with the object of displaying their sexual charms. We all dress to show off in one way or another. We also exhibit ourselves by showing off our personalities or our intellect.

To a certain degree, we're all Peeping Toms, too. Men enjoy looking at "girlie" magazines. Both men and women enjoy looking at attractive members of the opposite sex. In the larger sense, peeping—looking at something outside ourselves and receiving stimulation from it—permeates our culture.

Yet there is a difference between these impulses in people who are not emotionally disturbed and in those who are. The difference isn't in the act as much as in the attitude toward it.

For the "professional" Peeping Tom the act is an occupation, and one with important symbolic rewards. For the amateur, the man who occasionally "peeps," the act is rarely even a preoccupation. It's mostly a matter of opportunity, and the opportunity is not compulsively pursued.

The amateur Peeping Tom seldom goes on to more significant sexual offenses. But what about the professional? Is exhibitionism, Peeping Tom-ism, frottage, transvestism, and obscene telephone calling merely a way station along the road to rape? Do those who are emotionally disturbed progress from minor sex variances to major ones? If a man in a library zips open his fly, might he follow you out of there and rape you?

The Kinsey Institute's study of sex offenders says, "Our data may be interpreted to prove that sex offenders do not as a rule commit offenses of increasing severity. The hypothesis of evolution, from the trivial to the serious, is not a sound one."

The chances that the minor sex offender will do anything more annoying than he's already doing are just about nil—unless, of course, you go out of your way to antagonize him.

13

Children vs. Sexual Assault

It's one thing to teach a grown woman or even a teenager the psychological and physical defense she can use against a rapist, and quite another to impart the same information to a child.

Clearly, much of what we have discussed is far beyond the comprehension of almost any child below the age of puberty. Not only are the defenses too sophisticated for most children to understand, even the whys and wherefores of an assault are difficult, if not impossible, for a child to grasp. This presents a problem because children are raped and mutilated and sometimes even murdered. It doesn't happen as frequently as the news media would have us believe (actually, I'd guess that less than one rape in 30 involves a prepuberty child), but it does happen and when it happens, the victims are usually totally helpless. (Interestingly, more boys than girls are the victims of sexual attack.)

Children are also molested—touched, fondled or encouraged to touch and fondle an adult in a sexual manner

—and they're usually just as defenseless against these assaults. Furthermore, depending on how they perceive it, a child may be terrified by such an episode.

Traditionally, our society has had but one thing to say to children about rape or molestation and that has been the simple warning: "Stay away from strangers." I think that's the wrong thing to tell any child.

According to crime statistics and psychological studies, three-fifths of those times that children are molested or raped the perpetrator and child are *acquainted*. The rapist or molester is a friend, neighbor, relative or acquaintance. So telling a child not to go near strangers isn't enough, yet if you were to follow that line of logic, you'd also have to tell him to stay away from friends, neighbors, relatives and acquaintances—in fact, everyone. You might as well tell him to stay in his room and keep the door locked.

In addition, telling your child to stay away from strangers could implant a fear of people that will last him his whole life through. Whom does a child know when he's four years old, anyhow? Should he or she be afraid of everyone he's going to meet, including his teachers, his doctor, the policeman on the corner, his father's boss, the schoolbus driver, his piano instructor, the coach of his Little League baseball team, the great-grandfather he sees only once a year? These are only a few of the strangers he'll meet when he's a child and they are all people you want him to like, respect or trust, not fear.

Children can't know the difference between dangerous strangers and benign ones. More importantly, by telling your child to stay away from strangers, you haven't given him a defense. All you've really done is saddled him with a fear of people, a fear that could cost him dearly in the assault situation and in his development toward a well-adjusted maturity. If your child is terrified of strangers, and somehow meets up with one and finds himself in the assault situation, how will he react? Very likely by screaming, struggling, crying or running. As we have seen, this may be a very dangerous reaction.

In recent years I've heard it recommended that children be taught physical self-defense—karate and the like. A child can't learn enough self-defense for it to be useful, even if he knows *when* to use what he knows.

I recommend self-defense lessons for children only on two conditions: 1) that the parents find an instructor sensitive enough to teach their child both the skill and the wisdom necessary to use it, and 2) that this knowledge is combined with the psychological preparedness that can only come from understanding what an assault is. Otherwise, all he'll end up doing, if he uses his skills in an assault situation, is struggling—or what will be perceived as that by the assaulter. Even if the assaulter is taken off guard once and thrown by a very skilled child, you can be sure that he won't let it happen again. And, after being humiliated by a mere child, he may be furious, though it should be noted that child molesters usually use persuasion rather than force.

Rather than warning your child away from all strangers or making him depend on self-defense techniques, you should give a child at least a rudimentary understanding of mental illness or maladjustment so that he can recognize what might mean trouble. Without getting technical, without frightening him, give him some idea of what an assaulter or molester might do to him. Tell him how to react to a stranger who does things he shouldn't—without trying to teach the child complex philosophies or psychologies. Teach him what he should do in such a situation.

Most important, a parent should open a channel of communication with the child about matters like these—a permanent channel—so that if something does happen the parent will know about it and be able to say and do what is necessary. Deal with sexual matters with the child—whether or not we're talking about an assault—so that he has the best chance of growing into an emotionally healthy adult.

Begin with the concept of mental illness. Use his experiences as a basis for your explanations. By the age of five or so, your child has no doubt spent an evening away from home, perhaps at his grandmother's. Very likely he has felt homesick. Begin your conversation with him, at this age, by reminding him of that feeling.

"You felt bad," you might say. "You were sick inside and unhappy. Well, there are adults who feel sick in that way, too, and they feel that way all the time. They're probably more unhappy than you'll ever be. They're unhappy because they don't have friends, or because the people they like don't like them, or because they don't like themselves. And sometimes, they don't even know they're sick.

"People like this," you can continue, "need to go to a doctor, just like you do when you get sick. If you're homesick, seeing your Mommy and Daddy again is the same as going to a doctor. It makes you feel well."

The child can empathize with the adult who "feels bad inside," because he has felt this way. This is, of course, a vastly oversimplified description of mental illness and perhaps not entirely accurate, but it will do for our purposes. The next step is preparing him for what might happen if he comes across someone who's emotionally disturbed.

"You may never meet such a person. But then again, you may," you can tell your child. "And he could be almost anyone, someone you know or someone you don't know. People who are 'friend-sick' like this are very, very lonely. They're always looking for friends and they'll try to be friends with anyone, grownup or child. They have a funny way of trying to be friends: they put their hands on you and they want to touch you—on your knee, on your face, or on your vagina (or penis), or neck, or back or almost anywhere. Or they may want to kiss you, just about anywhere, and they may want you to kiss or touch them.

"Sometimes they won't stop if you want them to. They'll just keep touching. It's like when you're crying and I tell you to stop. You may want to, but sometimes you can't. The same goes for the friend-sick person who wants to touch you."

Now, at least, your child has some idea of what a molester might do to him, but he has it in a way that will lead him to feel empathetic toward the man, not terrified.

"This person, a man or a woman, may come up to you while you're playing someplace or maybe offer you a ride home from school. He may say he'll take you for a ride, or he may say he'll give you candy or buy you a present. He may even say that I sent him to pick you up, or that your mother (or father) did, or that he's your baby-sitter.

"But that's silly, isn't it? We would *never* send anyone to pick you up that you didn't know. And if I sent someone you knew, I'd tell you first, wouldn't I? So you can be sure anyone who tells you that I sent him or Mommy (Daddy) did is kidding, that he isn't telling the truth."

This, by the way, should be an inviolable rule in your household. It will automatically give your child confidence and trust in a certain set of relationships and cause him to avoid situations that don't square with customary arrangements.

"Now, I know it's nice to have someone give you candy or a toy or any kind of present. And sometimes it's fun to go on rides with people. When Mommy (Daddy) or I are with you, or we say it's all right, you can go right ahead. When we're not with you or we haven't said it's all right, it's not the same. The person offering you candy, or a toy, or a ride, or maybe even a trip to the zoo or an amusement park may be one of those people who are friend-sick. He may look fine, but he may be friend-sick.

"A friend-sick person who wants to give you something or do something nice to you is doing it so you'll be nice to him, so you'll let him be friends with you in that funny way where he touches you and maybe wants you to touch him back. The trouble with that isn't the touching, so much. I know you like to be tickled sometimes. It's that he may not stop when you want him to. Or he may touch you in a way you don't like."

It's too easy, I believe, to implant a fear of physical contact in a small child, a fear that in later life could make normal sexual relations disturbing or distasteful or even prohibitive. That's why I'm talking about touching as if it's essentially harmless and I'm not emphasizing the touching of any particular part of the body.

"Now, Bret (or Lauren, or whatever)," you might continue, "what should you do if someone offers you candy or a toy or a ride and Mommy and Daddy aren't around, or we haven't said it's all right?"

The child will probably say something like, "I shouldn't take it." If he does, tell him that's right. If he doesn't, lead him to that conclusion. This question technique is the surest way to make certain the ideas stick in his mind. It's also the surest way to know if there's real communication taking place between the two of you—if he's listening and he's understanding. For this reason, you should ask questions all along, to get him to restate what you're telling him in his own words.

"That's right, you shouldn't take it. Now what about a ride? Let's say you're playing in the school playground and someone offers to take you for a ride, maybe to the amusement park. Should you go?"

Lead him to a "no" answer.

"That's right. You shouldn't go. Instead, it's best to come home just as soon as you can, or go to your teacher or a policeman, or where other people are and tell them. I'll tell you right now that if someone like this offers you candy or a present or a ride and you come home and tell me, I'll make sure you get an even better present from me for being such a big boy (girl).

"Now the man or woman may tell you not to say anything about him to anyone. And he may try very hard to make sure you come with him. But the harder he tries to make sure you'll keep your talk with him a secret, and the harder he tries to get you to go with him, the more sure you can be that he's friend-sick.

"The best thing to do is to tell me or your mother (father) all about it, just as soon as you can, so we can make sure the man sees a doctor so that he won't be sick anymore. It doesn't matter if he doesn't want you to tell us. That's part of being friend-sick. He doesn't want anyone to know. But you'll be helping him if you tell us. And you won't make us mad. You haven't done anything wrong— it isn't the same as if you spilled or broke something or teased or picked on your little brother, or didn't act like a big boy (or girl)."

I want to emphasize that you should *never* give the child the impression that if he gets himself into this kind of situation he has done something wrong. That's the surest way to break the lines of communication between you and almost guarantee you'll never know what happened. Don't make your child feel that there's any great disgrace in having his body touched or in touching someone. Give it as little significance as possible. The parents who exaggerate this do their children a terrible disservice. The parents who keep their children in ignorance about sex are even more reprehensible. But those who instill fear are the worst.

"You know that not everyone who wants to be your

friend is friend-sick. In fact, you'll probably never meet someone who is. I just want you to know what to do if you do happen to meet a friend-sick person. If you don't know someone and he wants to be your friend, or if it is someone who's in high school or who's a grownup, or if you think someone you know is friend-sick, just come home and talk to me about it. I'm not talking about children your own age, of course. They're too little to be friend-sick. It's fine to make friends with any of them. It's probably fine to make friends with anyone else, too. Just come home first and talk to me about it.

"If you do find yourself with a friend-sick person, the thing to do is not to make him mad. Friend-sick people can get mad easily. Like you do when you have a temper tantrum. You know that sometimes you hurt yourself when you're having a temper tantrum, or you may break a toy. Well, if you make the friend-sick person mad, he might have a sort of temper tantrum, and he might hurt you, even though he doesn't mean to. That's why it's a good idea not to make him mad. Even if he touches you in a way you don't like.

"Of course, he won't touch you that way and he won't get mad at you unless you're alone with him. That's one of the things about a person like this. He wants to be alone with you. The best thing you can do is not to go alone with him. Go where there are other people. Stay with your friends. Come home as soon as possible.

"But whatever he does, don't start yelling or hitting or crying. That will make him mad. Remember, he's feeling bad. He's friend-sick and only a doctor can really help him."

It isn't enough, I believe, to tell a child not to scream or struggle. You have to give him a feeling of empathy for the disturbed adult, not a feeling of fear. The more you frighten your child, the more likely he is to react badly to a molester or rapist, and the more likely it is that he'll be seriously injured, or worse.

The language I've presented here is suitable for the comprehension of most five-year-olds. But you know your child better than I do. He may be able to absorb this at age four, or not until age six. Tell him when you think he can understand the ideas. Have him repeat what you say in his own words, so that you're certain he grasps what you're telling him. Repeat yourself then and there if there's any doubt. And six months from now, or maybe a year from now, tell him again.

There are other things you can tell your child that will protect him from molestation. You can protect him from obscene telephone calls by teaching him to ask, "Who is this?" whenever he picks up the phone. Don't let him stay on the phone, unless you know who's called, for longer than it takes him to get the caller's name.

Also, tell him never to open the door of the house to let anyone in except you or someone you told him was coming and should be admitted. If you hear someone knock or you hear the doorbell, don't let your child handle the situation alone. Supervise him closely.

Children also need close supervision when they're using a public rest room. These places are favorite spots for molesters, either heterosexual or homosexual. Small children, especially, should always be accompanied by a grownup they know when they use such facilities.

Another way to protect your child against molestation and against distorted concepts of sex is to start sex education as soon as possible. Just when, will depend on the child, of course. But I can tell you that if you wait until your child is in first grade, it's almost certain that he'll already be getting a sex education of sorts from his friends, and their knowledge may be full of errors of both fact and attitude. Your child may receive lasting false impressions about sex unless he learns the proper attitude and the proper facts at home.

I'd recommend that you get hold of (or have your local library obtain, if it doesn't already have a copy) *Education for Sexuality: Concepts and Programs for Teaching*, by Burt and Brower, published by W. B. Saunders, W. Washington Square, Philadelphia, Pa. 19105. This book discusses in considerable depth and detail a good way to introduce your child to factual sexual concepts.

If, despite the education and precautions, something does happen to your child, the odds are that it will be something minor. Lurid newspaper headlines to the contrary, the rape and murder of children is rare. Minor sexual incidents, however—molestation and some of the minor sexual annoyances I've talked about elsewhere—are fairly common.

Should your child have such an experience, *your attitude* toward the incident is more likely to have a lasting effect on him than the incident itself. Recent psychological research has shown that children who have been molested are rarely, if ever, "damaged for life" because of the incident. With few exceptions, when such children reach adulthood they show no higher rate of sexual disturbance than others in their social, ethnic and economic group who were not molested as children. The exceptions are those children whose parents overreacted to the incident in one way or another and treated it as a highly significant event, thereafter severely restricting the child's activities in order to "protect" him, or made the child feel guilty that he was involved in the episode.

There are many cases of this sort. After a lecture at a small, elite Southern women's college one evening, I spoke with a young woman who had been raped by her brother when she was ten and he was seventeen. As it happened, the brother was really a remarkable child, an outstanding scholar, athlete and musician. In short, he was everything parents dream of. One day, while this wonderful young man was wrestling with his sister on the floor, he pulled off her clothing and raped her.

At the time, she wasn't very disturbed. She had no idea of what had happened or what it meant. She'd been sheltered from such things and knew nothing whatever of sex, so she didn't tell either parent what her brother had done to her. She didn't *know* what her brother had done to her.

In the natural course of events, her mother finally gave her a book on where babies come from. She read it and soon went to her mother saying, "Mommy, this happened to me."

Her mother was unbelieving, then as she became convinced, thunderstruck. Her father was called in and he too was incredulous at first. His mood soon turned to fury. Finally, both parents talked to the brother—in the presence of the young sister. He admitted everything. The parents didn't blame the boy. Instead, they blamed her. She should have known better than to let her brother take her clothing off, they told her.

By the time I spoke to her, eight years had passed, but the girl, now a young woman, had evidently suffered ever since. Throughout her teenage and college years, she'd been unable to establish any kind of lasting relationship with a man. She hadn't really been able to get close to a man, even in a nonsexual way. The woman had one question to ask me and I could see how disturbed she was as she asked it: "Was I really to blame?" She wanted desperately to know from someone knowledgeable if her guilt was warranted.

Less than a month ago I came across another case where parental reaction to an assault might have been worse than the assault itself. A woman told me that when she was thirteen she'd been assaulted while leaving a dance. A man had leaped out from between some cars and tried to rape her. Fortunately, some friends came along and scared him off. When she came home and reported this to her parents, they reacted by completely closing down her social life. She was not allowed to date, to go to dances or parties or even school sports events. When I talked to her she was a freshman in college—a bright, pretty young woman who had never had a date in her life—who felt guilty for having been attacked. Guilt is probably the most difficult emotion to deal with. Once it's instilled, its ill effects are inevitable.

What was missing in both of these cases was a line of communication between parent and child. I can think of nothing more necessary, especially where sexual matters are concerned. The time to do this is when your child is young—before school begins, if possible. Sex education may provide the perfect opportunity. Don't make a big deal out of it. Just tell him that as he gets older there are things he should know and now he's old enough to know about how babies are made. The way to make that communication strong and long-lasting is to *accept* his or her feelings, whatever they may be—confusion, interest, indifference, fascination—and to be nonjudgmental. Communication means that *both* parties talk and both parties *listen* and both parties *understand*. And completed communication means that each party understands exactly what the other understands. When communication fails, it's usually because this last factor is ignored. In short, if you want to establish completed communication with your child in such a way that he will come to you and tell you when he's troubled about sexual matters or any emotional problems, the best way is to treat him as a human being rather than as a "mere" child.

Parents are laying the foundations of an emotionally healthy and happy sexual life for their children in later years when they build a strong communication link with them, teach them how to protect themselves against molesters without frightening the wits out of them, provide sex education to neutralize any erroneous information or impressions the child may have picked up casually, and react with understanding and a cool head toward any sexual mishap in which their child is involved.

Such parents do more than that. They also help assure that a new generation of sex variants doesn't come into being. They help reduce the rapist population and the number of those who commit minor sex annoyances by doing what they can to see that their own children grow up emotionally stable—well adjusted within the mores of our society. Being a good parent is quite a responsibility.

14

And If It Happens Anyhow

Let's say that despite everything you've tried to prevent it, you've been raped. And your assailant has left you lying, in shock, in the bushes. The first thing you'll probably do, after you've recovered some of your composure, is to take an inventory of your parts. If you're lucky or if you've handled the assault well, you haven't been harmed in addition to the rape. Possibly your clothing is in good enough shape that you can still cover yourself.

So you get up off the ground, wobbly, distraught, but still able to get home. The episode, terrifying and shocking as it was, is past. You've survived. The worst is over.

But the worst may not be over. For some women, there are experiences ahead directly connected to the assault that may be more devastating than the actual rape. Some of these may be brought on by their own behavior. All, in the end, are the fault of a society that has declined to understand any of the problems of rape.

In our society there's a cherished myth that when someone is injured in any way, he or she is entitled to, and gets, special treatment in the form of aid and comfort. This is certainly true of the senior citizen who's been mugged, the person who's suffering from a disease or the crippled child. Too often, it's not true in the case of a woman who's been raped.

Rape just happens to involve sex. And whenever there's sex, there are moral attitudes and judgments of every variety. People become concerned with what should have happened, rather than with what did happen. They react almost as if the double standard were on the statute books, not as though it was only a tradition of a still-adolescent society that refuses to practice what it preaches: that everyone is created equal.

As a result, many a rape victim is condemned, either outright or subtly, while her assaulter is sympathized with, "understood," allowed to plead guilty to a lesser charge, or let off. In my opinion, this is stupid, unfeeling and unjust in the extreme. It helps neither victim nor rapist. But that's the way it is, even in this enlightened age.

It is my sincere hope that these attitudes will change and society will become convinced that the victim of a rape is *truly* a victim, and in *no way* a perpetrator.

Meanwhile, however, you should know how to deal with society as it is. If you're raped, there are a number of possible ways you can react. The most important thing to remember is that you must act quickly and surely if you are to protect yourself from the mental and physical aftereffects of rape and from society's judgments, and if you are to have any chance of seeing that the rapist is treated the way he should be.

If you decide to keep the whole thing to yourself, you're going to have some problems you didn't have before. When you're raped, you suffer mental wounds. No woman—no matter how mature or sexually experienced, no matter what traumas she may have survived in the past—is immune to this. If you tell no one of your rape, you've practically guaranteed that your psychological wounds, minor or major, won't heal—*ever*. Even if the memory fades from your conscious mind, it will be buried in your subconscious and such a psychic skeleton in the closet will cause trouble, even when you think you've forgotten it entirely. For example, it may cause you to feel a deep, generalized and totally unconscious anger toward all men. This feeling could easily prevent you from establishing a satisfying, long-term relationship with a man, even if, in your conscious mind, you want one desperately.

Also, there may be physical problems as the result of being raped if you keep the experience totally to yourself. Obviously, you'd seek medical attention for any injuries you might have suffered in the assault, but if you ignore the rape itself, there is the possibility of contracting venereal disease or becoming pregnant.

Another major problem of keeping quiet about your rape is ethical: your rapist is still out there somewhere. He may be looking for another woman. By not speaking out, you're in effect allowing him the freedom to do as he wishes.

Unfortunately, few events in a woman's life could be more difficult to discuss, and for some women talking about what happened will be nearly impossible.

If this description fits you, and if your locality does not maintain a woman-staffed rape-crisis center, call the National Organization for the Prevention of Rape and Assault (NOPRA) in Manhattan (212)371-3664. They will be happy to talk to you and advise you. You need not give your name. If you wish, they'll put you in touch with a local guidance counselor, psychologist, physician, hospital or attorney who can help you further should you need more help. Or they'll make preliminary contact with the police to smooth your way, acting as an intermediary in *any* capacity you choose, being a sort of circuit breaker for you; any pain or abuse that could normally result from these initial contacts will be avoided. Or they'll just talk to you, for as long as you want, until you feel able to take further steps on your own, if that's your wish. Or the person you contact will just be an anonymous, empathetic listener who will always be understanding.

Whether or not you want to go to the police, I recommend that you see a doctor. Not only will he be able to treat your wounds if any, but he will also be able to give you a shot of penicillin to prevent V.D. and also a "morning after" contraceptive to help prevent pregnancy. He might also be the perfect person with whom to share the entire story, to air it out so that the mental wounds don't fester.

On the other hand, some doctors have been known to react unsympathetically to rape victims. It may be that they simply don't want to get involved or that they don't feel that the practice of medicine includes the care and treatment of rape victims. Perhaps such men have made moral judgments of their own, which wouldn't be surprising, since doctors are a part of society at large.

How do you choose the right doctor, then, if you elect that alternative?

Women I've talked to who've been raped say that just about the last doctor you should visit is the intern, resident or staff doctor at a clinic infirmary or hospital. These doctors are usually so busy that even if they are sensitive and sympathetic, they rarely have the time for you. Chances are, you'll get nothing more from them than a patching up plus a shot of penicillin and a "morning after" pill.

The physician most likely to treat you as a human being is your own family doctor or your gynecologist, or the family doctor or gynecologist of a friend if you're away from your hometown. His prior knowledge of you, either directly or through your friend, will lead him to consider your situation more sympathetically than he would if you were a total stranger.

Even if you decide to go to the police, a physician may be able to give you valuable additional help. He or his nurse could accompany you to the police station—which would serve the purpose of giving you emotional support if the police turn out to be hostile and unsympathetic (and, unfortunately, some are). Furthermore, the doctor or his nurse could serve as the next best thing to an eyewitness in supporting your claim that you've been raped.

Your doctor will be able to tell the police of your distraught and disheveled condition when you arrived at his office, of any sperm in your vaginal tract and of any bruises or wounds. He will be able to do this, that is, if you go directly to him following the rape. If you stop off first at home, douche, take a shower, change your clothing and put on a bandage or two, he won't have much to tell the local law enforcement people. The evidence will be gone.

For this reason, if you intend to go to the police, don't clean up first. This will go against your natural impulse, especially if you feel that your rapist has dirtied you—and you'll probably feel just that way. But you haven't a chance of being believed if you wash away all the evidence.

If you don't know any doctor in town, you may want to go first to a friend or relative, both to ask for the name of a doctor and to have company and emotional support when you make the trip to his office. Choose a woman friend who is as close to your own age as possible and who knows you well. Your father or mother may not be the right person to tell first. They might be inclined to make some moral judgments about what happened. But you know them better than I do. My point is that you should find someone empathetic whom you trust. This isn't the time to start arguing over whether one man can rape one woman.

This goes double if you're thinking of going first to your husband or boyfriend. Too many times the reaction is that you've done something wrong—not that something wrong has been done to you. This is true even of men who are well-educated and should know better. Sociologist Stephen Schafer of Northeastern University in Boston admits, "If my wife were raped, I don't know how I could forgive her—even though I am wrong."

A couple of years ago a rapist was arrested in Queens, New York. It turned out that he'd been responsible for eleven rapes. As soon as he was caught and eleven women identified the man, two of their husbands sought divorce. According to Helen Pastore, the police detective who helped solve the case, they said, "What do you mean, you were raped? Why did you let him in here? What do you mean, he had a knife? Why aren't you cut and bleeding?"

Can you believe a husband would prefer to have his wife cut and bleeding rather than just penetrated? This is love? I don't think a woman should have to show battle scars before someone believes she's been raped. But this view, unfortunately, isn't in the majority. Not yet.

If there is no sufficiently empathetic friend or relative available, you might consider going to a psychiatrist, psychologist, priest, minister or rabbi, or perhaps the dean of women at your school. Any one of these professionals would probably be happy to recommend a doctor and even accompany you to his office. They would all be happy to talk to you after you've seen the police, too, to give you the kind of emotional support you may find that you need.

Incidentally, when you go to the sex crimes analysis unit of your local police department, you don't necessarily have to prosecute your rapist. And don't think that just reporting it won't be useful. Your rape may be part of a pattern and may help the police to prevent other women from being raped.

Going to the police is not likely to be a pleasant experience, even if you're accompanied by a friend, relative, doctor, nurse or guidance counselor. (And I do *not* advocate that you go unaccompanied.) Male members of the police force don't necessarily have contempt for women or harbor rape impulses of their own. Very probably, they're not guilty on either count. But they, like most other men, are likely to be supporters of the double standard or they may have prurient interests. And by the terms of the double standard, if you've been raped and you're still alive, you're the one who has done something wrong—not the rapist. This is one good reason, by the way, to seek out a policewoman when you visit the station, even one who is not on the rape detail. She's more likely to understand your feelings. She may direct you to a sympathetic sergeant to make your report to or she may otherwise assist you. However, some women are as strong supporters of the double standard as men. So don't seek help *just* on the basis of sex. Look for a *person* who understands or wants to understand.

Some police recognize that many of their number have an antiquated attitude. New York detective Al Simon, of the Central Park District, says, "A lot of officers, especially the old-timers, believe that unless a woman comes in bruised, there's no rape. They also say, 'Unless a woman's a virgin, what's the big deal?' But I wonder: if one of these guys was suddenly jumped and forced to commit sodomy at gunpoint, wouldn't he be pretty upset? And wouldn't he submit?"

Policemen *have* seen many a false claim of rape, or else they think they have. Unfortunately, there *are* some women who cry wolf. I know of one case in which a woman was "pinned" to a man in a fraternity who broke off with her. The next day, she went to the police and said she was raped. The police weren't exactly overwhelmed by the evidence she presented, but one sergeant, who had a daughter about the same age, was convinced. He pushed and pushed and got the case up to the district attorney. A couple of weeks before the trial the young woman came to the sergeant and said that what really happened was that the guy wanted his pin back and she was trying to take her revenge. You can imagine what effect that had on the town police force—and on that particular sergeant.

According to police statistics, about 18 percent of all alleged forcible rapes every year are determined upon investigation to be falsely claimed. Among the reasons, according to the police, are jealousy; being discovered by parents, boyfriend or husband while in the act of intercourse; pregnancy or V.D. in a married woman who couldn't possibly have gotten either from her husband; childhood or teenage crushes coupled with rejection by the love object; or psychiatric troubles. I can't vouch for that 18 percent figure. In fact, I'd guess that the true figure is much lower. But I am willing to admit that some women do cry rape falsely, making it that much harder for the woman who is really raped to convince those in positions of authority that she's telling the truth.

To make the matter more complex, policemen, by the very nature of their jobs, see the dregs of humanity. They are accustomed to dealing with the worst sort of people: thieves, muggers, murderers. And they see women at their worst, as drunks or prostitutes or con artists, or when they're engaged in a family fight. Most of the women they see in the normal course of events probably don't elicit much respect, and given the human tendency to generalize, it isn't easy for them to shift gears totally.

I don't think the police should be condemned outright for their attitude, but whatever the reasons, you're not going to have a picnic in the police station if you've been raped.

According to the Boston Women's Collective, if you've been raped and you go to the police, "prepare to feel as though the police are raping you *again.*" The policemen who question you may insist on full details, including how the experience felt. More often than not, they may openly suspect you of having provoked the man and then changed your mind about submitting to him. Women have reported that the first thing the police asked them was, "Did you reach a climax?"

Such comments and the kind of police behavior we've been discussing are unprofessional conduct and the officer should be reported to a higher authority. The law enforcement officers I've discussed this matter with have all said that a woman does not have to put up with such treatment in the police station.

I can't tell you that you must go to the police if you've been raped. I can't tell you for sure that you'll help yourself by doing so. I can't even guarantee you'll be helping other women. After all, the man may not be caught. But I think that if you do have the guts to go to the police, it's all to your credit.

Incidentally, I believe that police attitudes toward rape are currently undergoing a change. In recent months I've often been approached, after lectures, by policemen interested in getting more information on the subject of assault. Judging by their questions, I'd say that they're showing more and more empathy for the rape victim. Police departments are setting up sensitivity training programs and are using women officers for rape victims unable to relate to male officers. New York City has an excellent program, which many other areas are using as a model.

Once you go to the police, your job will be done, unless the man is caught. In that case, you'll be called down to the station house to attempt to identify him. Even though you're the victim, not the defendant, I advocate that you consult a lawyer at this point. Remember, the district attorney represents the state. The defense attorney represents the rapist. Without your own attorney, no one represents *you.* And today the one person who needs protection in a rape trial is the woman. The police may be a little too informal about the identification procedure. You should have the opportunity to view a line-up in such a way that the suspects can neither see nor hear you. What you don't need now is another face-to-face confrontation with your rapist. Your lawyer can see to it that you're shown the proper respect.

After you've identified the man, his lawyer and the district attorney may try to make a deal—that he plead guilty to a lesser charge, for example—by throwing a scare into you about a "rape trial" with all its publicity. Your lawyer will be able to tell you what the chances of conviction are on the original charge.

Then, if you have the guts to see it through, you have my admiration. I've been involved as an expert witness in a rape trial and I can tell you that the defense attorney can be unmerciful to the woman. You see, he has one object: to defame the woman's reputation enough so that his client *couldn't* have raped her under any circumstances. He may call as witnesses past boyfriends who've made love to you, or someone who claims that you wear provocative clothing or walk in a provocative way. He may call in a neighbor who asserts you often have wild parties or come home at all hours of the night. Before the trial is over, you'll feel that you're the one being prosecuted, not your rapist.

Your problems, should you prosecute, don't end with what the defense attorney and his witnesses will say or imply about your character. The jury also presents problems. Both the men and women, I'm sorry to say, will be susceptible to defense arguments that you've somehow tempted the defendant into committing an act he never would have considered otherwise. Many times the women, judging you against their own "unblemished past," will be even harder on you. They may look at you with contempt, feeling that you somehow should have fought harder.

I remember one occasion in a small Midwestern town when a woman was so badly beaten during a rape that she was hospitalized, unconscious. And yet I heard one woman from that town tell another, when discussing the case, that the victim "could have fought harder." In fact, forty-eight hours after the rape, the victim died. How could she have fought any harder than to fight until she died? And still she was condemned.

Even if by some chance the defense attorney doesn't attack your character or your reputation is so immaculate that there's no way to besmirch it, you should remember that there are only two witnesses to the crime in most cases —he and you. Both of you will have to tell your story in open court. The man will probably deny or soften everything. When it's your turn you may find yourself having an experience second in horror only to the actual rape. Whether you're willing or not, the defense attorney will probably try to get you to tell exactly what happened, in the most precise detail imaginable.

Then, after all of this, there's still a chance—a good chance, I'm afraid—that your rapist will get off scot-free. Nationally, about 65 percent of all rape prosecutions fail each year.

Whatever the outcome of the trial, you'll suffer afterward. You may find that you're ostracized by some of your acquaintances, relatives and friends. Society can't seem to get over the notion that in rape the victim is somehow also the perpetrator. You may find that other women, especially, will believe that you encouraged your attacker in one way or another and that nothing you say will change their minds. You may find that men are taking a new interest in you, not because they're interested in forming a relationship, giving their sympathy or showing you that all men aren't bad, but because they're sure you're sexually easy.

It's not a pleasant picture, and I'm not trying to scare you out of prosecuting. However, you should have a realistic idea of what is involved. Actually, you should prosecute if you feel you can handle it mentally. But I do emphasize here that I personally do not put the burden of prosecuting on you. I feel you've gone through enough. Yet by prosecuting, you have a chance of getting the rapist off the streets. Even if he isn't convicted, his arrest record will make him a likely suspect when another rape is committed —and he might be convicted for that one. So the end result, if you prosecute, is that you may be helping an untold number of other women and possibly children.

Some changes must be made in what happens to a woman after she's been raped. Most of all, society must take a close look at what's happened and place the blame where it belongs. In the last decade or two, there has been some improvement in the area—on the order of about 2 percent. Maybe the day will come when no stigma is attached to the rape victim, but it doesn't look promising.

Still, there are some legal changes that could be made that would improve the situation dramatically. First, defense attorneys should be barred from asking questions about a rape victim's past, whether or not she has one. Do we allow defense attorneys to ask mugging victims if they've been mugged before? A woman's past simply doesn't matter if she's raped. Just as a virgin can be raped, so can a prostitute. All that's necessary for rape is that the woman be *unwilling*. It doesn't matter whether she's been willing before or willing afterward, or willing with a regiment of sailors or never willing with anyone. If she was forced to have sexual intercourse against her will, she was raped. Period.

It would also help if a woman didn't have to come in with cuts and bruises to prove she was unwilling. Women should not be told to do something in the assault situation that is going to get half of them raped, mutilated or worse, just so the other half can prosecute.

Most of the people who advocate screaming and struggling do so, they say, because, "How can a woman prosecute if she hasn't?" Under those circumstances, the hell with prosecution, then. It is much more important to get women home safely than to worry about the ease of prosecution.

A woman who has sexual intercourse against her will but submits to save herself from severe bodily injury or death is still raped. If she bears no scars, she shouldn't be penalized.

There is the problem of corroboration, however. I don't think that a woman should be able to put a man in jail simply by saying that he raped her. On the other hand, rape, by its very nature, is usually committed in private. There are rarely any witnesses. The answer here is very difficult, but it seems obvious that when a woman identifies a total stranger from a line-up, there can't be much doubt that a rape has been committed and that this is the man. When the victim knows her attacker, perhaps more investigation is necessary to determine the relationship between them. But even then, I'm not convinced that a witness should be required before the man can be convicted. Where are you going to find one?

We should also change the way we deal with convicted rapists. One of the reasons so few are convicted now—at least of what they're charged with—is that the penalties for rape are so severe. Juries are reluctant to send a man to prison for life or even twenty years when there exists in their minds the slight possibility the victim may have encouraged him even a little. If we've learned anything in the last three thousand years, we've learned that an emotionally disturbed person isn't cured by throwing him into a dungeon. The way the law and the courts work today, the man convicted of rape will spend a few years in prison, then be paroled and then go back out onto the streets again. A few years of being locked away with a thousand other men will not cure him of his problem. In fact, whatever sexual variance he lacks when he enters prison will be introduced to him there. There's a good possibility he may rape again, and this time more violently than before. After all, when he gets out, society's rejection of him will be that much more aggravated.

We have to take a whole new look at how to deal with a convicted rapist. Our aim should be to *prevent rape* rather than to take revenge. And I believe this to be true of all crime. The best way to stop the rapist from raping is to treat him psychiatrically. Discover his problems and attempt to solve them. It's either that or put him in prison for life and keep him there, and our society does not have the stomach for that. On the other hand, it may be willing, if enough legislators get enough pressure, to devise a rational, mandatory treatment program for the rapist. A long-term program combined with confinement in a hospital for several years seems to me the most rational approach, the one most likely to work, the one most likely to be accepted by society.

If we can settle on a rational way to deal with the rapist, a way likely to cure him of his emotional disturbance without subjecting him to a prison term guaranteed to make him even more emotionally disturbed than before, it will be easier to get convictions in rape trials, and we'll be taking another step toward preventing rape. Such a treatment will take the focus away from the victim and put it where it belongs—on the rapist.

With these changes—the prohibition of questions about the victim's reputation, dispensing with the need for witnesses (though in a way that preserves the defendant's rights), a rational treatment for rapists designed to treat the root causes of rape (his emotional disturbance or maladjustment) the destruction of the double standard and the resultant effort to treat everybody equally—I think that society's attitude toward the victim will slowly become more realistic and humane.

We must all work for this in whatever way we can.

Bibliography

Abrahamsen, D. A. "Study of 102 Sex Offenders at Sing
   Sing," *Federal Probation* 14 (1956), 26–32.
———. "A Note on the Theory of Perversion," in Sandor
   Lorand and Michael Balint, *Perversion: Psychodynamics
   and Therapy*, pp. 3–15. New York: Random House, 1956.
Alexander, F., and H. Staub. *The Criminal, the Judge, and
   the Public*. New York: Macmillan, 1952.
Amir, M. *Patterns in Forcible Rape*. Chicago: University of
   Chicago Press, 1971.
———. "The Role of the Victim in Sex Offenses," in
   H. L. P. Resnik and M. E. Wolfgang, eds., *Sexual
   Offenses*. New York: John Wiley & Sons, 1970.
Apfelberg, B.C., et al. "A Psychiatric Study of 205 Sex
   Offenders," *American Journal of Psychiatry*, 100 (1944),
   762–70.
Baker, H. M. "Sex Offenders in Massachusetts Court,"
   Journal of Social Psychiatry, 20 (1950), 102–7.
Bender, L., and A. Grugett. "A Follow-Up Study of
   Children who Had Atypical Sexual Experience,"
   American Journal of Orthopsychiatry 22 (1952), 825–37.

Bettelheim, B. *Symbolic Wounds*. Glencoe, Ill.: Free Press, 1954.

Blanchard, W. H. "The Group Processes in Group Rape," *Journal of Social Psychology*, 49 (1959), 750–66.

Bloch, H. A., and A. Niederhoffer. *The Gang*. New York: Philosophical Library, 1958.

Bowman, K. M. and B. Engle. "Certain Aspects of Sex Psychopath Laws," *American Journal of Psychiatry*, 14 (1954), 690–97.

Bromberg, W. *Crime and the Mind*. New York: Macmillan, 1965.

———. "False Accusation of Rape," *The American Journal of Sociology* 14 (1918), 539–59.

Buss, A. H. *The Psychology of Aggression*. New York: John Wiley, 1961.

California Sexual Deviation Research (progress report, 1952; final report, 1954). Sacramento, Calif.: State Department of Mental Hygiene.

Carter, L. F., et al. "The Behavior of Leaders and Other Group Members," *Journal of Abnormal and Social Psychology*, 46 (1951), 585–95.

"Comment: Police Discretion and the Judgment that a Crime Has Been Committed—Rape in Philadelphia," *University of Pennsylvania Law Review*, 117 (1968), 277–322.

Davidson, M. "Appraisal of Witnesses," *American Journal of Psychiatry*, 110 (1954), 481–84.

De River, D. *The Sexual Criminal*. Springfield, Ill.: Charles C. Thomas, 1956.

Drzazga, T. *Sex Crimes*. Springfield, Ill.: Charles C. Thomas, 1960.

Ehrmann, W. *Premarital Dating Behavior*. New York: Henry Holt, 1959.

Ellis, A., and R. Brancale. *The Psychology of Sex Offenders*.

Springfield, Ill.: Charles C. Thomas, 1956.

Eralson, D. A. "The Scene of Sex Offenses," *Journal of Criminal Law and Criminology*, 31 (1946), 190–92.

Festinger, L., et al. "Some Consequences of Deindividualization in the Group," *Journal of Abnormal and Social Psychology*, 47 (1952), 382–89.

"Forcible and Statutory Rape: Exploration on the Consent Standard," *Yale Law Review*, 62 (1952), 55–83.

Freud, S. "Beyond the Pleasure Principle," in *Collected Papers*. London: Hogarth Press, Vol. II, 1933.

———. *Group Psychology and the Analysis of the Ego*. London: Hogarth Press, 1933.

Gardner, G. E. "The Aggressive Destructive Impulse in the Sex Offender." *Mental Hygiene*, 34 (1950), 45–63.

Gebhard, P. H., et al. *Sex Offenders*. New York: Harper & Row, 1965.

Gilbert, C. C. "Rape and Sexual Perversion," in Peterson, et al., *Legal Medicine and Toxology*, vol. 1.

Group for the Advancement of Psychiatry, *Psychiatrically Deviated Sex Offenders*. Report no. 9, May 1949; revised February, 1953. Topeka, Kansas, 1953.

Guttmacher, M. S. *Sex Offenses: The Problem, Causes and Prevention*. New York: Norton, 1951.

Halleck, S. L. "The Physician's Role in Management of Victims of Sex Offenders," *Journal of the American Medical Association*, 180 (1962), 273–78.

Hollander, F. P., ed. *Leaders, Groups, and Influence*. New York: Oxford University Press, 1964.

Kanin, E. J. "Male Aggressions in Dating Relations," *The American Journal of Sociology*, 63 (1957), 197–204.

———, and C. Kirkpatrick. "Male Sex Aggression in University Campuses." *American Sociological Review*, 22 (1953), 52–58.

Karpman, B. *The Sexual Offender and His Offenses*. New York: Julian, 1954.

Kinsey, A. C., W. B. Pomeroy, and C. E. Martin. *Sexual Behavior in the Human Male.* Philadelphia: Saunders, 1948.

Kramer, D., and M. Karr. *Teen-age Gangs.* New York: Henry Holt, 1953.

Landis, J. T. "Experience of 500 Children with Adult's Sexual Relations," *Psychiatric Quarterly*, 30 (1956), 91–109.

Litin, E. M., et al. "Parental Influence in Unusual Sexual Behavior in Children," *Psychoanalytic Quarterly*, 25 (1956), 37.

Lorand, S., and M. Balint. *Perversion: Psychodynamics and Therapy.* New York: Random House, 1956.

MacDonald, John M. *Rape Offenders and Their Victims.* Springfield, Ill.: Charles C. Thomas, 1971.

Mead, M. *Sex and Temperament in Three Primitive Societies.* New York: New American Library, 1950.

Redl, F. "Group Emotion and Leadership," *Psychiatry*, 4 (1942), 573–96.

Reik, T. *The Psychology of Sex Relations.* New York: Rinehart, 1943.

Reinhardt, J. M. *Sex Perversions and Sex Crimes.* Springfield, Ill.: Charles C. Thomas, 1957.

Resnik, H. L. P., and M. E. Wolfgang, eds. *Sexual Behaviors, Social, Clinical and Legal Aspects.* Boston: Little, Brown, 1972.

Schafer, S. *The Victim and His Criminal: A Study in Functional Responsibility.* New York: Random House, 1968.

Schapper, B. "The Best Defense against Sex Perverts," *Today's Health*, 36 (1958), 28–29.

Sherif, M., and H. Cantril. *The Psychology of Ego-involvement.* New York: John Wiley & Sons, 1947.

Stekel, W. *Sexual Aberration*, vols. 1 and 2. New York: Liveright, 1930.

Stern, M. "Facts of Sex Offenses against Children." *Parents Magazine,* 29 (1954), 42–43.

Tappan, P. W. "Some Myths about Sex Offenders," *Federal Probation,* 19 (1955), 7–12.

Vincent, C. "Ego-Involvement in Sexual Relations," *The American Journal of Sociology* 65 (1959), 287–96.

Wile, W. F. "Case Study of a Rapist: An Analysis of the Causation of Criminal Behavior," *Journal of Social Therapy,* 7 (1961), 11–31.

Witman, H. *The Sex Age.* New York: Doubleday, 1961.

About the Author

FREDERIC STORASKA was born in 1942 in Bloomsburg, Pennsylvania. He attended North Carolina State University; during his junior year he witnessed and broke up the brutal rape of an eleven-year-old girl by a gang of teenage boys. Moved to study the phenomenon of rape by this shocking experience, he discovered it was a taboo subject, on which very little research had been done. Mr. Storaska made of himself the nation's leading expert on the understanding and prevention of rape in our society.

In February 1965, twelve weeks after he presented his first "rape-prevention program" at a private women's college in North Carolina, a young woman in a court trial for rape testified for the prosecution that her life had been saved by the information she received when attending Mr. Storaska's lectures. Since that time, he has lectured to more than a million people, and more than two hundred and seventy-five cases have been reported in which his program has prevented serious assault and/or saved lives. He has also made a movie of his rape-prevention program to be shown on television to high school students.

Mr. Storaska is the founder and executive director of the National Organization for the Prevention of Rape and Assault and consultant to the National Crime Prevention Institute.

He lives with his wife and children in Weschester County in New York.